Curiosities of Norfolk

A County Guide to the Unusual

by

Josie C Briggs

For Elisabeth

By the same author
Walks in the Wilds of Norfolk
Walks in the Wilds of Suffolk

Cover Photographs:
Front Top – Clock Tower Cottages at Little Ellingham
Front Bottom – Seahenge replica at Thornham
Back – Pyramid tombstone, Attleborough Cemetary

Published by John Nickalls Publications
ISBN: 1 904136 04 4

Printed by Geo. R. Reeve Ltd.
9-11 Town Green, Wymondham, Norfolk, NR18 0BD

ACKNOWLEDGEMENTS

I would like to thank the following for their help and information: Norfolk Wildlife Trust (Foxley Wood, Wayland Wood, East Wretham Heath); Watton Tourist Information (Clock Tower); the owners of the Seahenge reconstruction site; and the compilers of the many information sheets, booklets and websites that I consulted.

Huby Fairhead of the Norfolk and Suffolk Aviation Museum at Flixton, Len Bartram, Ken Jackson and Patrick Allen kindly supplied a great deal on information on Langham dome teacher, based on their own research.

My husband Andrew helped with research and visiting the curiosities with me, and managed to find new oddities even when we got lost in the narrow lanes.

I am especially grateful to Steve Benz for giving an unkown author a chance four years ago, and whose idea this book was.

ABOUT THE AUTHOR

Josie Briggs has lived in Norfolk since 1988 and has explored much of the county. She is particularly interested in the countryside, wildlife conservation and organc gardening, and her articles have been published in several magazines including *Organic Gardening, Suffolk and Norfolk Life, Country Gardens and Smallholdings, Amateur Gardening, Aquarist and Pondkeeper* and *The Countryman*.

Josie is also a tutor in science and mathematics.

CONTENTS

CROMER AND NORTH-EAST NORFOLK

WELLS-NEXT-THE-SEA, HUNSTANTON AND THE NORTH-EAST COAST

KING'S LYNN AREA

INTRODUCTION

Norfolk ancient and modern - and everything in between. That nicely sums up this book, which is a collection of geological features, natural phenomena, prehistoric remains, ruins, buildings, street art, church furniture, and much else that is interesting. Another collector of curiosities would no doubt have come up with a different set, and indeed I could have kept going for another twenty or thirty, but one has to draw the line somewhere.

Norfolk's history stretches back 10,000 years, when the glaciers of the last Ice Age melted. The great ice sheets altered the landscape, scouring and pressing the ground, depositing material carried from far away. The clear earth soon became covered with dense woodland, but this did not last long. Humans began clearing the forest for their farms and settlements, gradually converting it to moorland and heathland.

Throughout the centuries Norfolk has been colonised by Saxons, Danes, Romans and Normans, all leaving their mark. I had no problem finding artefacts from these ages to include in this book.

History is still being made, of course, and Norfolk also contains some fantastic modern architecture. In fact, around the turn of the millennium was an excellent time to explore this county and write this book, because of the many commemorative village signs, artwork and other features that suddenly appeared.

My husband Andrew and I had a great time finding and visiting curiosities. I hope the reader enjoys doing likewise, whether physically, or in the imagination while reading this book.

Josie C Briggs

(1) NORWICH
CHEQUERED GUILDHALL

Position and access: Gaol Hill, Norwich

OS map reference: TG 228084

The unusual black and white chequered design on the top half of the exterior west wall is thought to signify the chequer table over which Norwich citizens paid their taxes. Now home to the Norwich Tourist Information Centre, the Guildhall was built in the fifteenth century and was then the largest medieval city hall outside London. Every citizen was ordered to contribute to its construction, with either money or labour. It contained three courtrooms that were still in regular use up until the 1980s, when the new Crown and County Courts were built on Bishopgate. Prisoners were held in cells underneath the Guildhall.

The building's history is as chequered as its wall, and on more than one occasion it was nearly lost. Its roof collapsed in 1511, then in 1634 it suffered subsidence due to saltpetre mining. In 1861, controversial City Architect Thomas Barry built a police station on its south side, perhaps thinking it was a convenient place next to the courts and gaol. The latest threat came in 1908, when it was proposed to pull it down. Fortunately the Guildhall survived all these problems.

The Guildhall remained the city's seat of government for five centuries, until the modern City Hall opened nearby in 1938.

(2) NORWICH
BISHOP'S THRONE

Position and access: Norwich Cathedral,
                           Cathedral Close, Norwich.

OS map reference: TG 235089

This ornate wooden seat is the oldest bishop's throne still in use in England, and the only one of its kind north of the Alps. It was built in part by Bishop Losinga when the cathedral's foundations were laid in 1096. Two sections of carved stone, at least 1200 years old, beneath the seat were brought to Norwich from the original cathedral at North Elmham (see (68) North Elmham: Saxon Cathedral) by the Normans.

At that time Herbert de Losinga was Bishop of Thetford, a post for which he bribed William Rufus with £1900. His conscience was troubled and he confessed to the Pope, who ordered him to build the cathedral at Norwich and move the seat of the bishopric there. Losinga subsequently became first bishop of Norwich, but the great cathedral was not finished and consecrated until 1278.

Norwich Cathedral is spectacular inside and out. Its slender spire, ninety-six metres tall, is the second highest in England, after that of Salisbury Cathedral. The present spire and perpendicular roof were added after a lightening strike in 1483 caused a fire which destroyed the original wooden roof and spire. Other modifications have been made throughout the centuries, the most incredible being the placing of more than a thousand carved and painted bosses on the ceiling. These were ordered in the fifteenth and sixteenth centuries by Bishops Lyhart and Nix, and tell the story of the Bible from creation to the final judgement. Until recently you would have needed powerful binoculars to study these treasures, over twenty metres above your head. Now photographs of them all have been placed in a database, accessible to visitors via a computer near the entrance. It is worth browsing through some of these, marvelling at the bosses' detail and colours.

Outside, and connected to the cathedral, is the largest cloister in England, built over the thirteenth and fourteenth centuries, with parts of different styles according to when they were built.

(3) NORWICH

SAMSON AND HERCULES

Position and access:	Palace Street, Norwich, opposite the cathedral.
OS map reference:	TG 234089

These two strongmen hold up the porch of a night club door. The larger than life-size plaster statues have replaced the original stone versions, and make splendid guardians of the entranceway.

(4) NORWICH

MOTHER JULIAN'S CELL

Position and access: St Julian's Church, between Rouen Road
and King Street, Norwich

OS map reference: TG 235082

St Julian's Church, with its attached cell, was rebuilt after being almost totally destroyed by a wartime bomb. The church and grounds are now an oasis of calm in the busy city.

Mother Julian's cell is a reconstruction of the room where the saint spent much of her life writing and, according to some historians, ministering through her window to the spiritual needs of visitors. It can be entered from inside the church, and contains an altar and seats for quiet contemplation. The cell's exterior can be viewed from behind the church; go through the wooden gate on the left into the church grounds.

Julian (or Juliana; her real name is not known) was the first recorded English authoress, her most noted work being the mystical Revelations of Divine Love. Born in 1342, she lived as an anchoress, dedicated to living her life for God in solitude. She was probably connected with the nearby Benedictine nunnery on Carrow Road, which housed a library.

In 1373 she became very ill and was not expected to live. When she eventually recovered, she retired from the world into her anchorite cell, and wrote up the revelations she had received from God during her illness. She remained in prayer and contemplation for the rest of her life, and died in 1415. Mother Julian's religious writings are still highly regarded today.

(5) NORWICH
SUBWAY PAINTINGS

Position and access: Under the large roundabout where St Stephen's Road crosses the inner ring road.

OS map reference: TG 228080

Dozens of large, colourful paintings decorate the walls of this subway system. The pictures, all different, illustrate many aspects of Norfolk's history, tourist spots and everyday life. They were done several years ago by pupils of various schools in and around Norwich.

(6) NORWICH

BOOM TOWERS

Position and access:	Either side of the River Wensum, next to Carrow Bridge, King Street.
OS map reference:	TG 239077

These two ruined towers once were used to control traffic along the River Wensum. A chain suspended between the towers prevented boats from passing, but this could be raised to let a boat through by means of a winch housed in the tower on the south-west bank.

The Boom Towers are part of the thirteenth century wall that once encircled the city, enclosing a square mile of tightly packed housing. Over two miles of wall remains in sections, including several towers. A portion from Carrow Bridge to arched walls on Carrow Hill is practically intact and includes four towers: the two Boom Towers, Wilderness Tower and Black Tower. This section is now a protected relic. Wilderness Tower is on Carrow Hill and has an iron gate through which you can view the inside. Black Tower, so called because it is made of black flint, is larger and in better condition, and was built on top of the slope to give a clear view to the south. It was used as a detention centre for plague victims in 1665 and 1666.

Separate from these, Cow Tower stands on a bend of the Wensum to the north-east of the city centre and is so called because, after the walls fell into decay, it was used as a shelter for cattle grazing nearby.

Preservers of the walls and towers have a constant battle against plants trying to get their roots between the stones.

(7) NORWICH

SAINSBURY CENTRE FOR VISUAL ARTS

Position and access: University of East Anglia (UEA) campus. From Norwich Centre, take the B1108 towards Watton. The entrance to UEA is on the left at the city's outskirts; it is clearly signed.

OS map reference: TG 191074

This unique building houses a unique collection. Overlooking the woods, lake and river of the university grounds, the Sainsbury Centre is a strikingly modern structure of glass, metal and concrete. The partly underground Crescent Wing, designed by Sir Norman Foster and Partners, was added later.

The Centre houses the internationally important Robert and Lisa Sainsbury Collection of art, which was given to UEA in 1973. It also contains the university's Collection of Abstract and Constructivist Art and Design, including modern architectural models and furniture designs. The Crescent Wing holds a permanent display of 700 paintings and sculptures by Picasso, Moore, Bacon and Giacometti, together with art from Africa, the Pacific and the Americas. Some large Moore statues decorate the grass outside.

The Sainsbury Centre organises a programme of temporary displays and events, including family activities on the first Sunday of each month. There are a gift shop and restaurants. The building is accessible to wheelchair users, and disabled parking is available near the entrance.

The campus grounds, which are open to the public, contain a nature reserve, well maintained by the grounds staff. It contains a variety of habitats, including the river, the artificial lake, woods, marshes and a large hay meadow.

(8) NORWICH
ZIGGURATS

Position and access: University of East Anglia campus. For directions see (7) Norwich: Sainsbury Centre for Visual Arts.

OS map reference: TG 194074

These are the most unusual student residences I have ever seen. Called 'Ziggurats' by their architect Denys Lasdun, after a type of pyramidal temple built in ancient Mesopotamia, they were built in the early 1960s as part of an integrated design for the new university.

Design and construction of UEA began in 1960, and Lasdun, who also designed the National Theatre, was principle architect. All the university buildings are worth looking at for their originality. Lasdun also designed the massive 'Teaching Wall', raised walkways and the central square.

The concrete and glass buildings are best seen from the large hay meadow sloping down to the artificial lake by the River Yare. Over the years, many other buildings have been added to Lasdun's originals, all in keeping with the overall design. These include the spectacular Sainsbury Centre.

UEA stands on the east side of the Yare valley, on what was once the Earlham municipal golf course, donated by the city for the campus site.

(9) GREAT YARMOUTH
LARGEST PARISH CHURCH

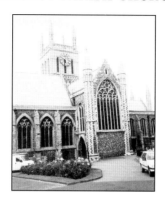

Position and access: St Nicholas' Church, Church Plain, Great Yarmouth. Walking from Britannia Pier, go north then take Euston road inland; this becomes St Nicholas Road. At the end, turn right. The church is on the right.

OS map reference: TG 524081

This is the largest parish church in England, and it is huge, dwarfing some cathedrals. It is 71 metres long, 34 metres wide, and has a floor area of over 2000 square metres. Its massive square tower is in the centre of the cross-shaped building, and there are numerous turrets with little spires all over the building.

The church used to be even bigger. It was built in 1101 by Bishop Herbert de Losinga, who also built Norwich Cathedral, and used to have twenty small chapels attached. During the Reformation, however, the chapels were pulled down, the church brasses melted down and ended up as the town's weights and measures, and the tombstones made into millstones. St Nicholas' also sustained damage during World War 2.

Inside is a pulpit in scale with the church, 3.5 metres long and 1.2 metres wide. Scenes from the Bible have been carved into its panels.

The church is normally kept locked, but a key is available from the Warden.

(10) GREAT YARMOUTH
NORTH-WEST TOWER

Position and access:	From Britannia Pier, head north along the coast, then turn left at Euston road. Continue until reaching the roundabout at the river, then turn right. The tower is on the east bank of the river.
OS map reference:	TG 522082

Great Yarmouth began as a temporary fishing village, dominated by Caister a few miles north. As the settlement developed from a few fishing huts in Anglo-Saxon times to a permanent town centuries later, conflicts and piracy developed with not only rival English ports, but also Dutch fishing fleets. Yarmouth began building its wall in 1284 to protect the whole town. The wall had fifteen towers, stretched over a mile in length and surrounded 133 acres by the river.

Quite a lot of the wall and some of the towers remain, now in ruins. The North-West Tower is one of the best preserved parts. It was erected by the townsfolk in 1344. Built of a variety of materials, from cobbles to bricks, the tower clearly had an extra storey added at some time, and it is obvious where the old wall was once attached. The ancient tower looks intriguing among the nearby modern buildings.

This tower has recently been refurbished and is now a Broads Authority information centre, well worth a visit when it is open during July to September.

Another well preserved tower is the North-East Tower, a little to the east.

The wall ruins can be followed for some distance parallel to the river a few blocks inland. It is amusing to see that one house has used a length of the town wall as one of its own walls, probably in the days before planning permission was required.

(11) GREAT YARMOUTH
NELSON'S PILLAR

Position and access:	From Britannia Pier, travel south along the coast road for about 1.5 miles. The column is on the right up a short side street, Monument Street.
OS map reference:	TG 529055

Although this column is dedicated to the Norfolk-born hero Nelson, the figure on top is not of the Admiral, but Britannia. The lady is not even facing the sea, but looking inland towards the docks and the River Yare. It is not known why this is so, but perhaps it is because Great Yarmouth was a river port, only becoming a seaside resort in the mid 1800s.

Situated near the docks away from the main holiday part of Yarmouth, this 43 metre high pillar was designed by William Wilkins after Nelson's death in 1805. It was raised by public subscription in 1819, over twenty years before the better known column in Trafalgar Square, London, was erected. The original Britannia figure, and six identical 'Victory' figures surrounding her podium, were made of artificial stone by Coade of Lambeth, but they were eroded by the salty wind and became dangerous, so were replaced with concrete copies in 1896. These also eroded and were themselves replaced in 1982 by more durable glass fibre versions.

The fluted tower contains a staircase and is open at certain times in July and August to the public, affording fine views over sea and town. Around the base are carved wreaths, the names of Nelson's sea battles, and an inscription: "Nelson, by birth, lineage and education. By mind, by manners and by disposition, Norfolk proudly boasts her own".

The 'Norfolk Heroe', as Nelson is called by local people, was born at Burnham Thorpe in north Norfolk. In Nelson's time, Yarmouth was an important naval base to which the Admiral returned after his victories in the Battles of the Nile and Copenhagen.

The monument is of national importance and its conservation and maintenance have been funded by Norfolk County Council and other sponsors.

(12) HOPTON

TWO ST MARGARET'S

Position and access: From Great Yarmouth take the A12 south towards Lowestoft. Turn off at Hopton on Sea. The new St Margaret's church is near the turn-off to the village. The ruin of the old St Margaret's is in the centre of the village.

OS map reference: TG 524000 and TM 530999 respectively

It is unusual to have two churches with the same name in the same village. The old church is now a Grade 2 listed ruin. The earliest record dates from 1090, concerning the appointment of a monk to read the services. St Margaret's served the farming and fishing villages of Hopton and Brotherton for over six hundred years.

On Saturday 2nd January 1865, the church stove overheated, set fire to the thatched roof and gutted the church. No time was wasted: in September of that year the foundation stone of the new church was laid. The replacement St Margaret's is not a copy of the old, but an imposing flint building with an octagonal tower.

On Easter Day of 1984, a large wooden cross was dedicated at the old church to commemorate more than six centuries of Christian worship there.

Leyline believers put the old St Margaret's church at one end of the longest known leyline in Britain, St Michael's leyline. This stretches four hundred miles from St Michael's Mount in Cornwall to Hopton in Norfolk, and passes through many historic sites including Avebury Ring and Glastonbury.

(13) BURGH ST PETER
PYRAMID TOWER

Position and access: St Mary's Church, about 2 miles east of Burgh St Peter village. From Lowestoft, take the A146 for several miles inland, then turn right at the roundabout on to the A143. After a mile, fork right and follow the convoluted road to Burgh St Peter. Go through the village and keep on the main road until it ends at the River Waveney. The church is unmistakable as you approach it.

OS map reference: TM494937

Although not a pyramid in the same sense as those at Attleborough and Blickling (see (79) Attleborough: Pyramid and (34) Blickling: Pyramid), this church tower is significantly wider at the bottom than the top. It consists of four brick cubes of decreasing size, stacked on top of each other like a pile of building blocks. The tiers were built in 1793, on the base of the original sixteenth century tower that collapsed in a storm. Perhaps the designer believed the new design would be more stable than the old on the marshy ground; it has certainly proved to be the case.

Like Attleborough and Blickling pyramids, the tower is a mausoleum. Several of the Boycott family were parish rectors over two centuries and were buried in vaults in the tower base. The first Rector Boycott, Samuel, paid for the present tower to be built on the base of the ruined one.

Surprisingly, the church is dedicated to St Mary rather than St Peter, although Blomefield's 'History of Norfolk', written in 1764, refers to it as St Peter's. When and why the re-dedication occurred is unknown. There used to be a smaller chapel nearby, known as St John's, but the ruin of this was depleted during World War 2, when its stones were used to repair local buildings.

The main body of the church is very narrow compared to its length, due to the chancel and nave being under one continuous roof. The church suffered another disaster in October 1996, when its thatched roof was destroyed by a blaze, thought to have been caused by a firework from a nearby display. It was soon repaired, with funding from English Heritage's Historic Churches Preservation Trust, and the Norfolk Churches Trust, although the parish still has to raise a substantial amount.

(14) GILLINGHAM

THREE CHURCHES IN A ROW

Position and access: From Beccles, Suffolk, take the A146 west
to Gillingham. The churches are north of
the village, to the right of the main road.

OS map reference: TM 412923

These are not in the same churchyard like those at Reepham (see
(57) Reepham: Three Churches in One Churchyard), but each standing
on its own ground. Like Reepham, one is a ruin and the other two
are sound.

The northernmost church is the oldest, and only the ivy-clad tower
and a small portion of wall to the east remain standing. The site is on
a mound overlooking the village, and young woodland is rapidly
taking over the churchyard.

Next door is St Mary's, a typical parish church with a square tower.

The southern church is a Roman Catholic, dedicated to Our Lady
of Perpetual Succour.

Each church is surrounded by its own graveyard. Our Lady's
churchyard contains a number of unusual wrought iron headstones.
Gillingham village sign is also of wrought iron, so perhaps there is,
or was, a local metal working industry.

(15) DUNBURGH
LAMP POST

Position and access: From Beccles, Suffolk, take the A146 west
to Gillingham, then take the minor road
westward to Dunburgh. The lamp post is
ahead as you approach a sharp right
corner, by a group of trees.

OS map reference: TM 404914

It would be easy to miss this because it is camouflaged amongst
trees of similar thickness and colour. The concrete post, minus its
lamp, looks older than the trees, so maybe it was erected to hold a
beacon or navigation light for the adjacent river, marshes, streams and
dykes. Once the Waveney was navigable as far as Bungay, which used
to be an inland port.

(16) RAVENINGHAM
METAL MILE POST

Position and access: From Lowestoft, Suffolk, take the A146, turn right at the roundabout on to the A143, and take the B1140 left. After 2 miles, turn left towards Raveningham. The pillar is on a bend shortly after leaving the southern boundary of the Raveningham Hall estate.

OS map reference: TM 392966

It is easy to drive by this black pillar in a shady spot. It stands around three metres tall and is made of cast iron, an octagonal turret set on a stone plinth. John Thomas Patience made it in 1831 for Sir Edmund Bacon. Most place names and distances have since eroded, but it is clearly 111 miles to London.

A plaque states that in MCMLXXXVI (1986 to you and me) the mile post was restored to commemorate Sir Edmund's birth.

Nearby Raveningham Hall and gardens are open to the public at certain times. The hall contains paintings by local artists Constable and Gainsborough.

(17) ASHBY ST MARY

SCULPTURED TOMB STONES

Position and access: From Norwich take the A146 south-east towards Lowestoft. At Hellington Corner turn left and follow the road to Ashby St Mary church.

OS map reference: TG 329022

Two tombstones in the churchyard are unusual because they are carved to show pictures of the deceaseds' occupation. Farmers George and Ann Basey lie side by side by the path to the church, flanked by their relatives' graves.

When Ann Basey died in 1868, aged seventy-one, her family erected a headstone sculpted with a picture of her in apron and bonnet, feeding the geese. The couple's thatched farmhouse is in the background, with her husband leaning on the fence watching her. George Basey died eight years later aged eighty-two, and his tombstone shows him feeding turkeys, again with the farmhouse in the background.

Presumably the Basey family were rich and influential in order to commission such gravestones, and to have a row in the churchyard all to themselves. They were not immune to tragedy, however: three grandsons died in infancy and were buried with their grandparents, one with Ann and two with George. All the boys were named Joseph Basey Fisher.

(18) SOUTH WALSHAM
GARAGE WITH A HOLY HISTORY

Position and access:	St Walsham Broad. From Norwich, take the B1140 north-east to South Walsham. Continue to Pilson Green, then turn left to the car park near the broad. The garage is across the road by the water.
OS map reference:	TG 372140

Many old chapels have been converted into houses, but this one has become a double garage. It is identified by the blue sign on its wall.

This very faded sign is barely readable, but you may just make out 'Parish Church of St Mary and St Lawrence'. Beneath the name is a map of South Walsham Broad and the surrounding area, with a 'You are here' marker. One gets the impression that this sign was not original to the church, but added later lest the church be forgotten.

On the roof at the other end of the building, there is an unusual weather vane, with a boat instead of the normal cockerel.

I do not know when and why the church closed, but maybe there was too much competition for worshippers. South Walsham is one of several Norfolk villages with two churches sharing the same churchyard (see also (57) Reepham: Three Churches in One Churchyard). These two parishes merged a century ago.

Nearby are Fairhaven Gardens, with many rare shrubs and other plants. The gardens go down to the waterside, where boat trips can be taken.

The lakes and dykes of Broadland are man-made, flooded pits and connecting channels, dating from peat excavations between 900-1300 AD. Broadland is now an important region for nature conservation and tourism.

(19) ST BENET'S ABBEY
WINDMILL IN A GATEHOUSE

Position and Access: On the banks of the River Bure, between
South Walsham and Ludham. From Great
Yarmouth, head north and by-pass Caister,
turn left and follow the A149 to Potter
Heigham, then go left again to Ludham. At
the cross-roads in the village, turn left,
then right. The Abbey is a mile walk to the
south. Alternatively, take a boat; there are
several places in the region where boats
can be hired, either self-drive or a guided
cruise.

OS map reference: TG 383157

The crumbling ruins of St Benet's Abbey were once a wealthy
Benedictine monastery, part of the estate of the medieval Bishopric
of Norwich. The monks who lived there were among the first people
to drain the marshes and build embankments to control the Broadland
rivers.

The monastery was founded in 1020 by King Cnut, and housed about twenty-five monks. It was very wealthy and owned properties in Ludham and other places. St Benet's was the only religious establishment to escape being dissolved by Henry VIII. William Reppes, the last abbot, became Bishop of Norwich in 1536 and was allowed to maintain St Benet's, but the abbey was soon neglected and local builders plundered it for stones.

An 18th century miller built a windmill in the remains of the abbey gate house. This is now also in ruins, having lost its sails years ago, but Norwich Castle Museum contains paintings by various artists showing how it looked in its heyday.

The present Bishop of Norwich is still the Abbot of St Benet's. Every year, on the first Sunday of August, the Bishop travels by boat to the ruined abbey and leads an open air service there.

(20) WOODBASTWICK

THATCHED PUMP HOUSE

Position and access: From Norwich, take the B1140 towards South Walsham. Almost a mile past Little Plumstead village, turn left at the crossroads to Woodbastwick. The Pump House is on the village green near the church.

OS map reference: TG 332152

This structure looks at first like a picturesque bus shelter, until you spot the machinery inside. It actually contains a well with a large iron wheel and handle to work the pump. This was the village water supply before mains water arrived. One of the interior roof beams bears the carved inscription: 'In memoriam Marguerite Tournois December 19th 1888'.

Thatching is still popular in Broadland, using local reeds. The neighbouring church of St Fabian and St Sebastian has flint walls, like so many Norfolk buildings, but a thatched roof, unusual for churches today. On the opposite side of the village green are two thatched cottages. The eaves of one of them bears the inscription: 'At evening time it shall be light'. Woodbastwick is an attractive village set around its green, hidden away in the lanes of Broadland.

THE JAWS OF HELL

Position and access:	St Benedict's Church, Horning. From Norwich, take the A1151 to Wroxham and Hoveton, then turn right at the A1062 to Horning. Go through the village, and turn right at Upper Street village to the church, which is well isolated from Horning village.
OS map reference:	TG 355166

This picturesque church of St Benedict, Horning, holds a grim secret. You need to go inside and up to the choir stalls to see some rare fourteenth century carvings on the bench ends.

The first one is on the near end of the left stall, and there is a small sign beneath: "Jaws of Hell (14th Century)". It depicts a fearsome scene of the devil pushing a sinner into a dragon's mouth.

At the altar end of the right stall is another carving, of two serpents biting another sinner. Presumably these sculptures were a warning of what awaited those who did not mend their ways! The altar end of the left stall has a carving of the earliest known version of the Arms of St Benet's Abbey.

It seems strange that Horning church is situated so far from the village, but it is actually in the centre of Horning Parish, which consists of Horning Lower Street (now the largest part), Upper Street, and Horning Hall to the east. The church once was part of St Benet's Abbey ('Benet' is an abbreviation of 'Benedict').

On approaching St Benedict's from the lych gate, it looks as though the church was built around a grand house, because the centre part is plastered and painted cream, while the tower and chancel at either end have flint walls. This is not the case, however, but is the result of the original north aisle being pulled down and its materials sold to finance roof repairs in 1749. The archways were filled in with a different material and covered with cream wash.

The churchyard is managed to encourage wildlife, with advice from Norfolk Wildlife Trust, and by the car park there are lists of wildflowers and butterflies that have been seen in the grounds.

HELTER SKELTER HOUSE

Position and access: On the bank of the River Thurne. From
Great Yarmouth go north along the A149
to Caister, then follow the road left to
Potter Heigham. Just before the River
Thurne, fork left and cross the narrow
bridge over the river. To reach the back of
the house, take the footpath behind the
chalets on the river bank. Or hire a day
boat from near the old bridge; you get a
better view from the river.

OS map reference: TG 418183

Set among the chalets lining the River Thurne is a most curious
round structure, looking like the top of a fairground helter skelter.
This, in fact, is exactly what it is, or at least was. It is believed that
a local bookmaker bought the structure and converted it into a holiday
chalet.

The village's name probably came from the pottery industry that thrived during Roman times. Near the River Thurne is an alarmingly low medieval hump-back bridge over the river. In the days when river transport was common, wherry masters used to lower their masts and pile stones on to their wherries to sink them low enough to negotiate the bridge. Now a pilot is employed by the boating companies to help holiday cruisers pass under the bridge.

The Museum of the Broads is located at Potter Heigham, housing a unique collection of traditional broads boats, tools and other items of historical interest.

(23) SUTTON

TALLEST WINDMILL

Position and access: From Norwich, take the A1151 north-east, then follow the A149 to Sutton. The windmill is east of the village.

OS map reference: TG 396239

    The UK's tallest windmill is now part of the Sutton Windmill and Broads Museum. It is a huge structure, with nine storeys, and visitors can enter and explore it. It is no longer working.

    The museum opened twenty-five years ago and contains exhibits of social life and everyday objects.

(24) CROMER

EUROPEAN BEACH PEBBLES

Position and access: The beach, Cromer

OS map reference: TG 213426 - 223422

At first sight Cromer beach looks like a typical pebbly shore. This beach, and those that flank it to the west and east, however, are particularly interesting because they are made up of a mixture of stones that originated thousands of miles away in mainland Europe.

The soft cliffs of this region date from the last Ice Age, which ended around 10,000 years ago. They consist of a variety of materials carried by glaciers, including rock fragments from Norway and sand, shells and flints from nearer parts of Europe. When the ice sheet finally melted, it deposited much of its material to form what is now called the North Norfolk Ridge, an attractive undulating part of the county.

If you look closely at the pebbles and rock fragments you may find, among the flint majority, pieces of pure white chalk soft enough to write with, mottled aggregates and other types of rock. Stones of many colours, patterns and textures are jumbled up on this beach. Rarely, you might come across a red-orange fragment of amber, fossilised resin from the ancient pine woods of continental Europe.

The crumbling cliffs along this coastline, particularly those between Cromer and Sheringham, contain many fossils, including bones of prehistoric elephants.

Cromer was originally a fishing village and is still famous for its crab fishing. It became a holiday town in the mid 19th century when the railway was built, and today is a popular seaside resort.

(25) SIDESTRAND

CHURCH SAVED FROM THE BEACH

Position and access: From Cromer, take the coast road (B1159) to Sidestrand. The church is on the left.

OS map reference: TG 260398

Although this church looks old, it was actually built early in the twentieth century - after Sidestrand's original church fell over the cliff in 1916! The present church was constructed using material from the old one. Its unusual eight-sided tower is a replica of the original.

This stretch of the north-east coast has been eroding away for centuries. Much of this area consists of low, soft cliffs and since the 16th century at least nine towns and villages have been swallowed by the North Sea. Shipden, near Cromer, was one which has completely vanished. According to local legend, when a storm is imminent, the ghostly tolling of Shipden church bells can be heard beneath the waves.

Sidestrand is one of several villages teetering on the cliff edge. Neighbouring Overstrand also lost its church to the sea, centuries ago. St Martin's church, Overstrand, was built in the 14th century to replace the earlier church. This church also has an eventful history. In the 18th century St Martin's fell into disrepair, and Christ Church was erected in the same churchyard. Early last century, the older church was restored, then Christ Church was pulled down after the last war.

(26) MUNDESLEY

RADAR DOME

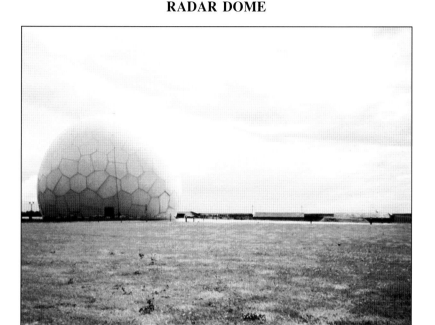

Position and access: Beacon Hill, near Mundesley. From
Cromer, take the B1159 coast road east
towards Mundesley. The dome is just past
the turn-off to Gimingham, on the right of
the road - you cannot miss it.

OS map reference: TG 284387

This spectacular white dome on the cliff top belongs to the
Ministry of Defence. You cannot approach it too closely, but can view
it clearly through the wire fence.

(27) WEST RUNTON
BEESTON BUMP

Position and access: From Cromer, take the A149 coast road west towards Sheringham. The Bump stands between East Runton and West Runton, on the right by the shore.

OS map reference: TG 197429

In a county noticeably lacking in hills, this little mound stands out clearly against the shore line. Its official name is Wood Hill, but locals give it the more colourful name of the Beeston Bump. It is named after nearby Beeston Regis village and heath, although the Runtons are nearer.

The Bump is an artefact of the last Ice Age (see also (24) Cromer: European Beach Pebbles, and (74) Thompson Common: Pingos). The soil and rocks of this region were carried here by the ice sheet from Norway and other far off regions. When the ice melted, it deposited its load as ridges and mounds; there are several "hills" scattered over the coastal region west of Cromer, but Wood Hill is by far the most prominent of these.

(28) SHERINGHAM

ROBIN FRIEND

Position and access:	West of Sheringham on (or under) the beach. From Sheringham Station, walk along the main street to the beach, then turn left and follow first the promenade, then the cliff top path for almost a mile (care: keep to the marked path and do not stray near the crumbling cliff edge). Alternatively, walk along the beach. Choose a time around low tide for your walk.
OS map reference:	TG 143437 to 148437

The seas along this stretch of north Norfolk have for centuries been eroding the cliffs and moving sand and shingle eastwards. Part of the beach between Sheringham and Weybourne to the west is at times completely scoured by the waves, exposing the chalk bedrock that underlies much of the county. This white shelf is exposed as the tide goes out, and if you choose your time of visit carefully, you may see the chalk gradually exposed, a great surprise if you are not expecting it.

When we visited ten years ago the chalk was exposed and easily visible from the cliff top. Recently we returned to photograph it and found most of the chalk had been covered by a few centimetres of sand and gravel washed on to it from recent cliff falls. A few high spots protruded above the shingle, and more bedrock could be seen clearly beneath the shallow waves. Robin Friend seems to be one of those features that appears and disappears, so you take your chance if you wish to see it.

It is not known who "Robin Friend" was, or why the chalk shelf was named after him.

Sheringham, like many other coastal towns, began life as a part-time fishing village. Like neighbouring Cromer, it became a holiday resort during Victorian times when the railways spread, making long distance travel much easier. It is still popular with holiday makers.

(29) UPPER SHERINGHAM
REPTON'S TEMPLE

Position and access:	The grounds of Sheringham Hall. From Sheringham, take the B1157 inland to Upper Sheringham village. Park either in the village, or follow the signs to Sheringham Park car park (charge). A short uphill walk, following the marked footpath, brings you to the temple.
OS map reference:	TG 138419

This graceful hexagonal folly, made of Portland stone, overlooks Sheringham Hall and the North Sea. On the information boards it is called Thomas Upcher's Temple. This is because the original designer, Repton, never saw his temple actually built. The temple was designed in 1812 but not built until 1975.

Abbott Upcher, aged twenty-six, bought Sheringham Hall estate in 1811 for 50,000 guineas. He commissioned Repton to design the temple, but suddenly died in 1819, before he had a chance to build the temple. His wife was too heartbroken to carry out his plan for building the temple.

The estate trustees built the temple in 1975 as a seventy-fifth birthday present for Thomas Upcher, a descendant of the Abbott. The position and design were modified. Originally the temple was to have been sited a short distance away, but it was actually built higher up away from the woods, perhaps because of the better view. Repton's design was circular, not hexagonal, to be built of brick infilled with flints.

ROUND RESERVOIR

Position and access:	From Sheringham, take the B1157 inland to Upper Sheringham village. The Reservoir stands in front of the church.
OS map reference:	TG 144419

You may hear this curiosity before you see it, because water gushes noisily through two overflow pipes into drains. The Reservoir, which used to be the village's main domestic water supply, is circular and surrounded by a flint and brick wall just over a metre high on average. The water flows out under an arch into a horse trough. A stone above the arch is carved with the legend "Anno Pacis MDCCCXIV" (1814).

The Reservoir, a Grade II listed building, is fed via a pipe from a spring. The inscription commemorates the end of the Napoleonic Wars, but the sculptor was over enthusiastic because the following year Napoleon escaped from exile on Elba and made a brief comeback, before being defeated and exiled a second and final time.

It was not until the mid 1950s that mains water came to Upper Sheringham.

(31) BEESTON REGIS HEATH
STONE HILL

Position and access:	From Sheringham take the A149 coast road east towards Cromer. Turn right into Beeston Regis; Stone Hill is on the left on leaving the village. It is quite steep to climb here. An easier way to reach the top is to park at Roman Camp to the east and walk through the woods and heaths for just under a mile.
OS map reference:	TG 171418

High viewpoints are in short supply in the relatively flat county of Norfolk. In fact, perusing through the OS maps, Stone Hill is the only one I could find. Stone Hill is a fine vantage point, with views over the north coastline and the North Sea beyond.

Stone Hill is part of the undulating Cromer-Holt Ridge, one of the most beautiful parts of Norfolk. It is the high spot of Beeston Regis Heath, the western end of 167 acres owned by the National Trust. The eastern end of this land is known as Roman Camp, although there is no evidence of Roman occupation.

At the top of Stone Hill is a stone pillar topped with a plaque showing what may be seen in the distance. There is also a welcome seat from which to enjoy the view. The coastal towns of Sheringham and West Runton are spread out below, and to the north-east is the curious mound of Wood Hill, or Beeston Bump as it is known locally (see (27) West Runton: Beeston Bump).

The soil and rocks of this region were transported from thousands of miles away by glaciers during the last Ice Age, then dumped here to form ridges and mounds when the ice melted. The top of Stone Hill is open heathland with low scrub, and it is covered by beautiful wildflowers in summer. It needs constant management to prevent colonisation by trees.

In the nearby woods there are several shallow pits dating from medieval times. These were used for smelting local iron ore, and slag from this industry may still be found in some of them.

(32) HOLT
MILESTONE AND MEMORIAL LAMP

Position and access:	Holt town centre, by the A148 Fakenham to Norwich road.
OS map reference:	TG 076387

Either one of these structures would be interesting in its own right, but they are sited close together in a prominent place, making an unusual pair.

The large milestone, known as the Holt Obelisk, is the oldest of the two and is quite worn in places. On each of its four sides is a list of seven places, with distances of up to forty-one miles away. The stone is topped by a pineapple sculpture. Local legend says that the pillar used to be a gate post at Melton Constable Hall, and that Sir Edward Ashley, MP for the region, donated it to Holt in the mid eighteenth century.

The jubilee memorial lamp, commemorating fifty years of Queen Victoria's reign, is actually a replica dating from 1992. The 1887 original was removed from the Market Place in 1920, to make room for the war memorial. Holt History Group and Holt Town Council commissioned the replica, which was made by Tony Sizeland, a Fakenham wrought iron worker. The lamp is called 'Blind Sam', but no one seems to know why.

Holt is an attractive Georgian town, mostly rebuilt after a great fire in 1708. There has been a settlement here from at least Saxon times.

(33) LITTLE BARNINGHAM
WOODEN SKELETON

Position and access: Little Barningham Church. From Aylsham, take the B1354 towards Holt. Just past Blickling Hall and its grounds, turn right to Itteringham, turn left and go through the village. Pass Mannington Hall on the left, then turn left towards Little Barningham. The church is on the right just before entering the village.

OS map reference: TG 142334

Little Barningham Church, constructed of flint like so many buildings of this region, is set on a mound overlooking the village and surrounding countryside.

This innocuous looking church contains a most weird and gruesome pew. It is on the left at the front, and you cannot miss it because there is a carved wooden skeleton, with hour glass and scythe, perched on one corner.

The pew is of the type that is completely enclosed by low wooden panelling with a gate by the aisle, the only one like it in the church. Carved lettering on the outside, well worn and difficult to read, states that the pew was installed in 1867 and intended only for "couples in wedlock". The inscription under the shrouded skeleton includes a poem beginning: "As you are now, even so was I, Remember death for ye must die".

(34) BLICKLING

PYRAMID

Position and access: In Blickling Park. From Aylsham, take the
road to Blickling, go past the Hall and
grounds, turn right then right again to
Itteringham Common, then right to a car
park. Follow the woodland paths about
half a mile to the mausoleum; a map in the
car park shows the way.

OS map reference: TG 166296

This is a much earlier pyramid than the one in Attleborough
cemetery (see (79) Attleborough: Pyramid) - and much larger. It is
the mausoleum of John Hobart, 2nd Earl of Buckingham, who died
in 1793 in mysterious circumstances, and his two wives Mary Ann
and Caroline. According to Horace Walpole, the earl "suffered from
gout in his foot, dipped it in cold water and so killed himself" (quote
taken from the Blickling Hall guide book).

The pyramid is an imposing monument, hidden behind conifer woods, in a large rectangular clearing, towering 13 metres above the rough grass. Built in 1794 by keen Egyptologist Joseph Bonomi, it is the largest and finest pyramid in England. An imposing portico at the front bears the family coat of arms, while at the back is a large plaque with an unidentifiable stone animal (bull or deer?) standing on a ledge above it. The plaque states that the pyramid was erected in Hobart's memory by his widow Caroline, and by William Asherton Harbord who married Caroline, daughter by Hobart's first wife Mary Ann.

John Hobart, grandson of the duelling Henry Hobart (see (35) Cawston: Duel Stone) became Earl in 1756 and had a long and distinguished career. He was Ambassador to St Petersburg between 1762 and 1765, and Lord Lieutenant of Ireland until 1780.

Blickling Hall itself, now a National Trust property, is a Jacobean hall in extensive grounds which include formal gardens, a lake and woodland area. Anne Boleyn's family lived in the original moated house. Sir Henry Hobart bought the estate in the seventeenth century and refurbished and expanded the old house to create the present building.

(35) CAWSTON

DUEL STONE

Position and access:	Side of B1149, east of Cawston. From Aylsham, take the B1145 towards Cawston and Reepham. Turn left at the cross-roads towards Norwich; the stone is on the right in a grove of trees just after the petrol station.
OS map reference:	TG 153241

This stone urn on a plinth sits in a grove of oak trees surrounded by a hedge. Owned by the National Trust, it is reached via a gate next to an NT information board.

The stone commemorates a duel fought on Cawston Heath, 20 August 1698 during the reign of James I, between Sir Henry Hobart of Blickling Hall and Oliver le Neve of Great Witchingham Hall. Incredible as it seems today, the neighbours' quarrel was about "words spoken in the heat of an election", according to the NT's plaque. The fight was probably illegal because Le Neve, the victor, fled to Holland after mortally wounding Sir Henry, who died next day at his home Blickling Hall. Lady Hobart and friends of the family put a price of £500 on Le Neve's head. Later Le Neve felt safe to return to England, stood trial but was acquitted by Grand Jury of any blame for Hobart's death.

The urn and the land it stands on were presented to the National Trust in 1964 by the National Benzole Company.

(36) BOOTON
CATHEDRAL OF THE FIELDS

Position and access:	From Aylsham, take the B1145 to Cawston. Turn left just past the church, then right. St Michael's Church is by the road on the left.
OS map reference:	TG 123224

This amazing parish church would look more at home in the middle of a cathedral city, yet it stands in a field by a quiet country lane. Its exterior is decorated with twin towers and many pinnacles, while inside there are great wooden angels hovering on the ceiling high above.

Dedicated to St Michael the Archangel, the church was designed by Whitewell Elwin, Booton's rector for fifty years, who had no architectural training. He borrowed ideas from buildings around the world, including Glastonbury Abbey, Venice and Egypt. Limestone was brought from Bath and black knapped flints from Mundesley beach to build the church.

Unfortunately, maintaining such a large building became increasingly difficult for a small parish, and the church became redundant in 1987. It is now cared for by the Churches Conservation Trust, and occasional services are still held there.

As well his day job as rector, Elwin edited the Tory journal Quarterly Review. He received so much editorial correspondence that the Post Office installed a letterbox at the church for him.

(37) WELLS-NEXT-THE-SEA
INLAND SEASIDE TOWN

Position and access: The Quay (B1105), Wells-next-the-Sea

OS map reference: TF 917438

    Wells-next-the-Sea is not next to the sea at all, but a mile inland. Norfolk's coast between Hunstanton and Salthouse is slowly being built up. Silt from outflowing rivers over the centuries has constructed salt marshes and mud flats, etched by outflow channels. Once important medieval ports like Wells and its neighbours are now more than a mile inland.

    Wells beach, separated from the sea by a mile of mud and marshes, is situated near the former harbour, which is now a boating lake with the picturesque name of 'Abraham's Bosom'. Wells is the only harbour of the region that still has an active trade. Local whelk and shrimp boats land their catches at the quay and coasters from mainland Europe exchange their cargoes for cereals. Huge warehouses, dating from the eighteenth and nineteenth centuries, loom over the quayside road.

If you wish to see the sea, you can either drive, walk or take the miniature steam railway. However, there is still no guarantee because low tides take the sea out a considerable way over the flat shore. The road ends at the lifeboat station, and a belt of pines, planted to stabilise the sandy soil, stretches several miles to the west. The pleasant walk along the waterside is part of the long distance Peddars Way and Norfolk Coast Path.

The mudflats and marshes of this stretch of coast are rich in bird and plant life, and much of the area is owned and preserved by the National Trust, Norfolk Wildlife Trust and other conservation bodies.

(38) BLAKENEY POINT
SAND AND GRAVEL SPIT

Position and access:	North Norfolk coast. From Wells-next-the-Sea, take the A149 eastwards to Blakeney. Blakeney Point is on the shore beyond the town. It can be reached by walking from Blakeney or Cley Beach, or by ferry from Blakeney or Morston when the tide is in.
OS map reference:	TF 989458 to TG 047454

Norfolk's coast between Hunstanton and Salthouse is being built up and outwards. Silt from outflowing rivers has constructed salt marshes and mud flats, and westward-flowing sea currents have shifted sand and shingle to form spits and islands. Three and a half miles long, Blakeney Point is the longest and most prominent sand and shingle spit in Norfolk.

The end of the spit, with the shore opposite, is owned and managed as a nature reserve by the National Trust. Much of this region is important for breeding and wintering birds. Blakeney Point supports colonies of breeding terns and other birds, and is a paradise for bird watchers. Common and grey seals can be seen here, especially if you go by boat. There is also a variety of shingle plants, many of which have deep roots which help stabilise the ground against scouring tides.

Salt marshes and mud flats, partly covered by high tides and channelled by rivers, have developed in the shelter of the spit.

Blakeney town was an important port in medieval times but now its quay on the Glaven estuary can only be reached by small boats. There is an information centre at Morston quay which can provide more information on the region.

(39) BLAKENEY

LIGHTHOUSE TOWER

Position and access:	St Nicholas' Church, Blakeney. From Wells-next-the-Sea, take the A149 coast road eastward to Blakeney. The church is easily visible, on a high spot overlooking the town and coast.
OS map reference:	TG 033436

Like several other small towns of this coastal region, in medieval times Blakeney was an important port. Wealth generated by the wool trade was used to build large Norman "wool churches". Eventually, however, the rivers silted up and cargo boats could no longer reach the ports, which became landlocked. Only small boats can now reach Blakeney quay.

Many coastal churches had navigation beacons on top of their towers. Blakeney church is the only one to have a separate tower for this purpose, a smaller square tower at the north-east corner, at the opposite end of the building to the large square bell tower. Openings at the top let out the light, and sailors used the beacon to navigate through the channels around Blakeney.

(40) LANGHAM

DOME TEACHER

Position and access: On the site of the old Langham Airfield.
From Wells-next-the-Sea, take the A149
coast road east. At Stiffkey turn right, then
fork left towards Cocksthorpe and
Langham. The old airfield lies on the far
side of Cocksthorpe, and the dome teacher
is on the left of the road.

OS map reference: TF 994419

This unusual building is an old "dome teacher", also known as an
"astrodome" on the site of Langham Airfield, a World War 2 air base.
Langham dome, and the control tower now converted into an office
and stores, are the only remaining airfield buildings. The airfield was
sold in 1961 and the site is now mostly farmland and turkey sheds,
but in 1945 two thousand service personnel were stationed here.

There is some debate about the dome's actual history and usage, but the following is believed to be the most likely.

The dome was probably built in 1943 when the airfield was temporarily closed for rebuilding work. Seven and a half metres high, and twelve metres across at the base, it was designed as an anti-aircraft simulator, where gunners could practise shooting down enemy aircraft projected on to the inside surface. The trainee's experience could be made more realistic with appropriate lighting and sound effects.

When Langham Airfield re-opened, the dome was fitted out to train Coastal Command Beaufighter crews, based at the airfield, to drop torpedoes. There was a flight simulator device in the centre and the airmen "flew" this and practised dropping virtual torpedoes at images of enemy warships projected on the dome's inner skin.

In October 1944 the Beaufighters left and Wellingtons arrived at Langham, and the dome was adapted to train air-to-air turret gunners. Bomb-aimers also used dome teachers to practise bomb-aiming, by sitting on a framework and aiming at a moving target projected on to the floor, but it is not known if Langham dome was used for this purpose.

After the war, the dome may have been used for its original purpose of anti-aircraft trainer, and after that to train navigators in night-flying, by projecting the stars on to the inside of the roof, hence the alternative name of astrodome.

It was originally planned to construct twenty-five dome trainers across the UK, but around forty were eventually built. It is not known how many were built in Norfolk, or if Langham dome was the only one. It is certainly the only dome still standing in the county.

A group of enthusiasts is hoping to restore the dome and possibly open it to the public, but at the time of writing it is not certain when or whether this will go ahead. The dome is a scheduled ancient monument, so any restoration work must be authorised by English Heritage and will be very expensive.

(41) BURNHAM NORTON
WINEGLASS PULPIT

Position and access: St Margaret's parish church is nearer to Burnham Market than to Burnham Deepdale. From Wells-next-the-Sea, take the A149 coast road westwards. Go through Burnham Overy Staithe and turn left at the next crossroad towards Burnham Market. The church is on the right.

OS map reference: TF 834428

This unusual pulpit, no longer used, is the finest wineglass pulpit in England. Set on a slender stem, it consists of six painted panels. At the front is St Jerome, who was a Secretary of the Roman See in the fourth century. The painting is not an accurate likeness because the large Cardinal's hat he is wearing did not exist until after his death. Other saints depicted are St Ambrose, a fourth century Bishop of Milan; St Gregory, a sixth century Pope; and St Augustine, Bishop of Hippo, North Africa around 400 AD. These four saints are collectively known as the Four Latin Doctors, respected theologians who set out the early Christian doctrines.

The two rear panels nearest to the rood screen are portraits of John and Katherine Goldale, who donated the pulpit to the church in 1450. Unusually, the donors' pictures are the same size as those of the saints, instead of much smaller as was normal practice.

St Margaret's is one of many churches in Norfolk to have a Saxon round tower (see also (65) East Lexham: Oldest Saxon Round Tower), although the main body of the church was rebuilt later. As well as the pulpit, it contains an unusual Norman square font, and a restored fifteenth century rood screen. On some of the interior walls are fragments of wall paintings, probably dating from the fifteenth century.

(42) BURNHAM DEEPDALE
CARVED FONT

Position and access: From Wells-next-the-Sea, take the A149 coast road westwards. St Mary's Church is in Burnham Deepdale village, on the right.

OS map reference: TF 804443

Long before gardening magazines existed, with their 'Jobs for the Month' sections, the inhabitants of Burnham Deepdale could go into their parish church and consult the font. On three sides of the square Norman font are twelve carvings, four per side, showing a gardening task for each month. An information notice on the wall tells which each labour is: they include digging, pruning, weeding, mowing, and pig slaying. The font's west side is carved with the tree of life.

The font once stood in the north aisle. When it was moved in 1797, the base was broken and so the font was taken to the Rectory at Fincham for repair. Either the workman was very slow, or the Rector liked the font so much that he kept it in his garden for forty years.

The font is made of Barnack stone from Rutland. The four legs are replacements for the damaged ones, and are believed to be a good copy of the originals.

Like many churches in Norfolk, St Mary's has a Saxon round tower (see also (65) East Lexham: Oldest Saxon Round Tower). The church was extensively refurbished in 1797, 1855 and 1898. Despite all this work, the south and west walls are probably the original Saxon walls built at the same time as the tower.

The stained glass windows comprise a particularly valuable collection of medieval glass. A leaflet is available for purchase in the church describing the glass, the pulpit, and other interesting features.

(43) HOLME-NEXT-THE-SEA

SEAHENGE RECONSTRUCTION

Position and access: From Hunstanton, take the A149 north-east
through Holme. The timber circle is in the
corner of an orchard on private land.
Access is with the owner's permission, via
the farm shop on the left of the road
between Holme and Thornham.

OS map reference: TF 721433

The original Bronze Age timber circle was removed from its site
on the beach (OS reference TF 693442) for study and preservation,
shortly after its discovery. This beach at the mouth of the Wash is a
Site of Special Scientific Interest, of international importance for its
wildlife. This coast is unstable, having been re-shaped by the sea over
thousands of years. In 1998 winter storms washed away a protective
sandbank, and the tops of the timber circle were exposed for a few
hours at every low tide.

Studies showed that the circle is four thousand years old. It was soon dubbed 'Seahenge' because of a passing similarity to Stonehenge, although much smaller. When built, it was several miles inland, but coastal erosion and rising sea levels eventually submerged the site. The fifty-five oak posts encircling an inverted oak tree were buried under sand and preserved. Its purpose is not known.

Exposed to the elements, the timber would soon have rotted away. English Heritage originally intended to leave the circle in place, but later were persuaded to remove the timber to a safe place to preserve this valuable Bronze Age relic. There was much controversy about this decision. The wood was transferred to Flag Fen Laboratories near Peterborough, and stored in water tanks to prevent further deterioration. The laboratories here specialise in the study of prehistoric timber.

Marks from tools on the wood, unique for timber of this age, provide information on the wood-working methods of the time. This led Channel 4's Time Team to reconstruct the circle using Bronze Age tools and methods. The programme went out in December 1999, and itself caused controversy over the felling of the required oaks. All was sorted out, however, in the end.

The reconstruction is visible from the road behind a hedge, but for a good view you need to take the path behind the farm shop (with permission), and perhaps treat yourself to some delicious fruit from the shop.

(44) HUNSTANTON
COLOURED CLIFFS

Position and access: From Hunstanton town centre, head
                           towards the beach and follow the coast
                           road northwards to the end of the
                           promenade.

OS map reference: TF 672413 and northwards

   Norfolk's coast has an interesting geological history, with parts
eroding away and other silting up. Perhaps the most surprising, and
certainly the most colourful, section of coastline is found at the north
end of Hunstanton at the mouth of the Wash. These 18 metre (60 ft)
cliffs are remarkable not only because the shoreline on either side
consists of sand dunes and saltmarsh, but because of their coloured
layers.
   Seeing the cliffs for the first time is a bit of a shock, because their
vivid stripes are even brighter than those found at Alum Bay on the
Isle of Wight. These cliffs are a Site of Special Scientific Interest,
managed by the Borough Council of King's Lynn and West Norfolk
in partnership with English Nature. An information board describes
the history and geology of the cliffs.

The coloured layers are due to sediments laid down when this region was intermittently covered by prehistoric seas between 70 million and 125 million years ago. Subsequent earth movements lifted the hardened layers to form land, and later erosion by the sea exposed the layers.

The lowest and thickest layer consists of orange-brown carstone, a type of sandstone riddled with tiny pebbles and stained brown by iron oxide (literally rust). Above the carstone is the thinnest of the three main bands, a rare red chalk limestone deposited after the sea rose again to cover the sandstone. This bright red layer contains many fossils. The top layer is white, made of chalk limestone deposited at a later era when the climate here was tropical, like that of the Bahamas today. This too contains fossils, mostly of tiny plants and animals which once lived in the warm sea.

Like many Norfolk coastal towns, Hunstanton was a small fishing village before the coming of the railways in the 1860s. Landowners saw the opportunity to attract Londoners, and built the holiday resort by the beach south of the cliffs.

(45) HEACHAM

POCAHONTAS SIGN

Position and access:	From Hunstanton, take the A149 south to Heacham. The town sign is on the right of the main road.
OS map reference:	TF 684374

Why is a Red Indian princess commemorated on the sign of a Norfolk town better known for its lavender? The reason is that Pocahontas (1595-1617), daughter of Indian chief Powatan, married John Rolfe at Heacham Hall in 1614. In her portrait on the sign she wears the costume of an English noblewoman. She also has a memorial in the church.

English adventurer John Smith reported that she twice saved his life when he was at the mercy of her tribe. She was baptised as a Christian in 1612, taking the name Rebecca, and moved to England to marry. Sadly she died young of smallpox, leaving one son.

(46) KING'S LYNN
CUSTOM HOUSE

Position and access:	King Street on the east bank of the River Great Ouse, King's Lynn. The Custom House/Tourist Information is clearly sign-posted from the town centre.
OS map reference:	TF 616199

Designed by Henry Bell and opened as a merchants' trading centre in 1695, King's Lynn Custom House was described by the architectural historian Pevsner as "one of the most perfect buildings ever erected". Made of Stamford limestone, it is indeed a fine building standing proudly by the waterside. Sir John Turner, a wealthy wine merchant, alderman and Member of Parliament, commissioned and financed the building, and lived next door to it.

It became the official Custom House in 1703 after the Council declared the old Custom House in the Market Place to be "decayed and ruinous". In 1717 the Crown purchased the house for £800, and it remained in use as the Custom House for almost 300 years, finally closing in 1989 when HM Customs and Excise moved to their East Anglian central office in Ipswich. The building was restored in 1999 and opened by the Prince of Wales. It houses the Tourist Information office and a museum.

Still called the Custom House even though it isn't, the three-storey building has keystones depicting Bacchus the god of wine and Ceres the goddess of agricultural fertility, both representing important trading goods.

Originally there were an obelisk, ball and figure with a weathercock on top of the roof, but this was damaged during a great gale in 1741. The archways were filled in 1742, and there have been several other alterations over the years.

This building was Henry Bell's first major commission in King's Lynn, and the townspeople were so impressed that they hired him to design several more buildings in the town and surrounding area, including the Duke's Head Inn and North Runcton Church.

CHAINS AND KEYS

Position and access: The Old Gaol House, King's Lynn town
centre.

OS map reference: TF 617202

There are many interesting historic buildings in King's Lynn (see
also (46) King's Lynn: Custom House), and the old Gaol House is
one of them. Large chains and keys hanging above the door symbolise
this building's original use. It was built in 1784 to house the town
gaoler, replacing an earlier gaoler's house. The incumbent lived on
the job, with the prison yard and cells directly behind his house.

Later, the house was used as a police station until 1954.

(48) WOLFERTON

ROYAL STATION

Position and access:	From King's Lynn, take the A149 north. At Sandringham Country Park turn left to Wolferton.
OS map reference:	TF 660285

For more than a century, this little station was used by royalty visiting nearby Sandringham House. Now it is a museum, and the railway line has been dismantled.

Prince Edward (later Edward VII) bought the Sandringham estate in 1862, and he and his family travelled there by train to Wolferton Station, two miles away. The present buildings were designed for Edward and Alexandra in the 1890s, and were comfortable enough to spend several hours in and take rest and refreshment before completing their journey. The last royal train came here in 1966, after which the station was neglected and became derelict. The King's Lynn to Hunstanton line closed in 1969.

Wolferton station was almost demolished to make way for a housing estate, but this plan fell through. The station and yard were bought from BR by Eric and Herta Walker at an auction. The new owners lived there, restored the station to its original splendour, including the red carpet on the platform, and opened it as a museum. It includes Queen Victoria's travelling bed, made for her in 1828, and Edward VII's decorated toilet.

(49) WEST NEWTON

ORNATE WATER TOWER

Position and access: From King's Lynn, take the A149 north. At Babingley on the edge of Sandringham Country Park, turn right to West Newton. The water tower is on higher ground beyond the village.

OS map reference: TF 705278

This ornate and colourful structure stands on private ground but can be viewed from a considerable distance away. Maybe it was designed to look attractive for the inhabitants of Sandringham Estate, especially visiting royalty.

(50) ANMER

BOY SCOUT AND ROMAN SOLDIER

Access:

Anmer village sign. From King's Lynn, take the A148. Just past Hillington Hall turn left and follow the B1153 through Flitcham. Go left at the crossroad to Anmer.

OS map reference: TF 743294

Like many other Norfolk towns and villages, Anmer boasts a carved wooden sign made by Harry Carter. A schoolmaster and skilled wood carver, he began to make signs in the 1950s when some villages decided to commemorate the Queen's coronation with new signs. This was especially popular for villages in the vicinity of Sandringham Royal Estate, as Anmer is.

Anmer sign was, as stated by a brass plaque fixed thereon: "Presented to Her Majesty the Queen by Norfolk Boy Scouts, 1957", in gratitude for the support which she has given to the movement. The sign is unusually tall, with a scout depicted on one side and a Roman soldier on the other. Both sides have the Scouts' motto in Latin: "Este parati" (meaning, of course, "Be prepared").

(51) GRIMSTON

THE ROCKET

Position and access:	St Botolph's Church, Grimston. From King's Lynn, take the B1145 west to Gayton, then turn left to Grimston.
OS map reference:	TF 722219

At first sight St Botolph's Church looks typical of those of this region, flint and stone with a square tower. On closer inspection you should notice an unusual buttress on one corner near the tower. With flanges at the bottom and a conical roof, the buttress resembles a rocket, and so locals have named it the Grimston Rocket.

Botolph was a seventh century saint who baptised converts in nearby springs. Inside the church are medieval choir stalls carved with dragons and mermaids.

OBELISK

Position and access: For directions to Grimston see (51)
                            Grimston: The Rocket. The obelisk stands
                            in front of the church.

OS map reference: TF 722219

This unusual village sign was erected in 2001. It stands three metres tall, and was designed by cabinet maker Andy Willis and builder Russell Bowlby. It took two years to make and cost £3000.

The front of the pillar is inscribed with 'MMI Grimston'. The rear is carved with a progression of images showing the village history, starting at the bottom with footprints and ending at the top with a personal computer. Thirteen year old villager Tim Packer selected the images from entries in a competition held among local children.

(53) FAKENHAM

STREET ART

Position and access: Fakenham town square near the memorial.

OS map reference: TF 918297

This is one of several millennium memorials in Norfolk. Set in the pavement at ground level are two massive cast iron rectangles made up of thousands of letterpress characters. At one end of the square stand three unusual street lamps, resembling inverted fountain pens.

The blocks and lamps are street art designed and made by leading artist Simon Watkinson, furniture designer Robert Kilvington and blacksmith artist Matthew Fedden. Inspired by the local printing industry, they are part of a scheme to enhance Fakenham, completed in August 2000.

Fakenham dates from Saxon times and has some attractive historic buildings, including the parish church with its imposing fifteenth century tower.

(54) LITTLE WALSINGHAM
VILLAGE PUMP

Position and access:	From Fakenham take the B1105 north towards Wells-next-the Sea. At the crossroads go ahead, through East Barsham and Houghton St Giles to Little Walsingham. The pump is in the centre of the village.
OS map reference:	TF 933368

In any other village this curious small building would be a main attraction, but here it is mentioned in passing as "the pump". It is about 400 hundred years old.

It is much larger than most village pumps, consisting of a circular building with a door, presumably to allow access to the pipes and tubes. On top is a beacon; perhaps this was one of the first street lamps, or maybe it was lit on special occasions.

Little Walsingham is better known for its Shrine of Our Lady. Walsingham has been visited by pilgrims since the Middle Ages, when the wife of Richeldis, lord of the manor, dreamed that the Virgin Mary appeared and asked that a replica of the House of the Annunciation be built in the village, on the site of a spring. The Holy House rapidly became famous and pilgrims from all over the realm visited 'England's Nazareth'. Religious houses, hostels for pilgrims, merchants' premises and other commercial ventures were built around it during the following centuries. The Augustines founded a priory here in 1149. In its day, Little Walsingham rivalled Canterbury as a destination for pilgrims.

The complex was ravaged during Henry VIII's Reformation and very little of the original buildings remain.

In 1931 Reverend Hope Patten, Anglican vicar of the parish, began reconstruction of the Holy House, using bricks instead of wood. This new Holy House is now contained in a large church which displays a replica of the original Virgin image. At least 100 000 pilgrims visit the Shrine every year.

(55) LITTLE SNORING

DETACHED TOWER

Position and access:	From Fakenham, take the A148 towards Cromer. Just past Alethorpe Hall, turn left to Little Snoring. The church is at the far side of the village, on the right.
OS map reference:	TF 953326

St Andrew's church, Little Snoring, is one of only two churches in England with its tower separate from the main building. This is an example of Norman re-building of a Saxon church, although it is not known why the Normans erected their new church a small distance from and out of alignment with the old round tower (see (65) East Lexham, Oldest Round Tower, for information on East Anglia's round towers).

Markings on the east side of the tower show where it was joined to the original Saxon church. An eroded gargoyle protrudes over the tower door.

The church is interesting inside as well as out, having a splendid Norman font.

Little Snoring is near the famous Thursford Collection of fairground organs, well worth a visit if you are in the area.

(56) BRININGHAM
BELLE VUE TOWER

Position and access: From Fakenham, take the A148 north-east towards Holt. At Little Snoring, fork right on to the B1354. Turn left at the crossroads towards Briningham. The tower is visible over the field to the right.

OS map reference: TG 035336

     This five-storey circular tower, now a private residence, was built in the sixteenth century, probably as a look-out or beacon tower. Its octagonal first storey is dated 1721, but the rest was probably added later, and there have been changes since. In its time the tower has been used as an observatory in the eighteenth century and a signalling tower during both world wars.

     The tower is at the far side of the village, on the right.

(57) REEPHAM

THREE CHURCHES IN ONE CHURCHYARD

Position and access: From Fakenham, take the A1067 south-east
                         towards Norwich. At Bawdeswell turn left
                         and follow the B1145 to Reepham. The
                         churches are in the town centre.

OS map reference: TG 102228

There are several examples in Norfolk of two churches sharing
the same churchyard at parish boundaries, but at Reepham there are
three. The towered churches of Reepham and Whitwell stand end to
end, but the third, Hackford church, is in ruins, having burned down
in 1543. It was not restored - maybe the villagers decided they had
enough churches for their needs.

St Mary's church, Reepham, is the most easterly and is the one
now in use. To the west, and joined to St Mary's by a common vestry,
is the smaller church of St Michael's; this contains a splendid Jacobean
wooden pulpit. Strangely, St Michael's church and surrounding ground

are detached from its old parish of Whitwell; this is unique among shared churchyards. The heavily overgrown remains of All Saints, Hackford, lie to the south-west and you have to explore the churchyard to find them among the trees.

The three parishes have now become one, that of Reepham. The connecting vestry of the surviving churches was added when the parishes united in 1935. The two churches were originally much smaller, but were expanded to accommodate increasing congregations in medieval times, until they eventually touched, overlapping at one corner.

Shared churchyards are exclusive to England's eastern counties. There are twelve known examples in Norfolk, four in Suffolk and odd ones in Cambridgeshire, Essex and Lincolnshire. In most cases one of the buildings is in ruins, or at best disused. The reasons for building two churches, or three in the case of Reepham, are not known, although legends and speculations abound.

(58) REEPHAM

HOTEL SUNDIAL

Position and access: Centre of Reepham (for directions from
                          Fakenham, see (57) Reepham: Three
                          Churches in One Churchyard).

OS map reference: TG 102231

Sundials are fairly common on churches, but this fine example is
found above the decorative doorway of the Old Brewery House Hotel,
built in 1728.

Reepham itself is a charming small market town, with narrow
roads and interesting shops. Many of its buildings, like the Hotel, date
from the eighteenth century. The old station is now a Museum of
Shops, with a penny-in-the-slot amusement arcade, exhibitions, gift
shop and cafe. You can hire bicycles from the museum to ride along
the local lanes and former railway track, the Children's Discovery
Ride, or the Safari Ride.

(59) FOXLEY WOOD
NATURAL SCULPTURE

Position and access:	Foxley Wood Nature Reserve. From Fakenham, take the A1067 south-east towards Norwich. Turn left at Foxley, go 2 miles towards Themelthorpe; the car park and wood are on the right. The reserve is closed on Thursdays.
OS map reference:	TG 054228

In the centre of this old coppiced wood, there stands an incredibly gnarled, old silver birch tree. When it was a sapling, it spiralled up round a honeysuckle which left imprints on the trunk that grew with the tree.

This natural sculpture has outlasted most of the man-made sculptures placed in the wood in 1991. The Norfolk Wildlife Trust (NWT), who own and manage the wood, commissioned six artists, Lorna Green, Richard Bray, Christine Fox, Rosemary Terry, Bee Springwood and Dale Rowe, to produce artwork out of natural materials that would harmonise with their surroundings. A few years later, most of the wooden sculptures had decayed and returned to nature, but there may still be traces of some for the observant visitor to find.

Foxley Wood Nature Reserve, covering about 300 acres, is a patch of ancient woodland that has been coppiced for timber for thousands of years. During the twentieth century the wood was abandoned and became overgrown, and much of it was replaced by a conifer plantation in the 1960s. The NWT bought the remaining woodland in the 1980s and has returned it to its former state by commercially coppicing the trees to provide timber products. This management regime opens up the woodland and encourages wildflowers and woodland creatures. The reserve is spectacular in late spring when bluebells and other flowers carpet the ground.

JUBILEE CLOCK TOWER

Position and access: From Fakenham, take the A1067 towards
Norwich. The clock tower stands at the
crossroads with the B1110 at Guist.

OS map reference: TF 997256

This splendid flint clock tower stands alone on a triangular traffic
island. A stone plaque on it tells how the tower was "Erected by
Thomas A Cook Esqre MP, JP, to commemorate the 25th anniversary
of the accession to the throne of their majesties King George V and
Queen Mary. May 6th 1935".

(61) WELLINGHAM
LEYLINE MARKER STONE

Position and access: From Fakenham take the A1065 south-west towards Swaffham. Past South Raynham, turn left to Wellingham. The stone is by the porch of St Andrew's church.

OS map reference: TF 871223

This curious boulder consists of a different type of stone from that used to build the church. Enthusiasts believe it marks a leyline that also runs through St Andrew's church at Little Snoring (see (55) Little Snoring: Detached Church Tower), Beacon Hill near Fakenham, St Martin's at Hindringham, and St Andrew's at Field Dalling.

In his book 'Timpson's Leylines', John Timpson recounts how he attended Wellingham church for years without giving the boulder second thoughts, until a parishioner told him the leyline tale and inspired him to investigate further.

ST WITHBURGA'S WELL

Position and access:	St Nicholas' churchyard, centre of East Dereham.
OS map reference:	TF 985133

According to legend, this spring appeared at St Withburga's original burial site, after her remains were removed to Ely. The water was believed to have healing properties, although it now looks decidedly unhealthy and dingy.

The transfer of Withburga's bones was not undisputed, and a plaque on the tomb describes what heppened: "The ruins of a tomb which contained the remains of Withburga, youngest daughter of Anna, King of East Angles, who died AD 654. The Abbot and monks of Ely stole this precious relic and translocated to Ely Cathedral, where it was interred near her three royal sisters, AD 974."

Withburga's father, King Anna, reigned over East Angles from 635 until he was slain with his son in 654, in a battle against the pagan King Penda of Mercia near Blythburgh, Suffolk. The royal family were pious people. Anna founded Blythburgh monastery and sponsored the monastery at Burgh Castle. He had several sainted daughters: Ethelreda, wife of the King of Northumbria, founded a convent and was abbess at Ely, and his eldest daughter Sexburgh became Queen of Kent and became Abbess of Ely after her sister's death. Withburga continued in the family tradition by founding a convent at East Dereham. After her burial in the churchyard, it is said that miracles happened at her shrine, which became a place of pilgrimage, bringing prosperity to the town. Locals regarded her as their local saint.

When the Abbot of Ely wanted Withburga's remains moved to Ely Cathedral to rest with her father's and sister's bodies, unsurprisingly the Dereham people objected. The only way he could get them was by using unholy stealth, abetted by a gang of Ely monks. In 974, Abbot Brithnoth and his monks visited Dereham and got the town leaders drunk during hospitalities. The monks exhumed Withburga's bones and escaped by boat, chased by the men of Dereham. Perhaps as divine compensation, a healing well sprung up from Withburga's desecrated grave.

St Nicholas' church is built in the shape of a cross with a central square tower. Despite the tower being large and apparently sturdy, it was too weak to hold the bells. A separate, larger tower was built in the grounds for the bells. This tower aso doubled as a gaol. A plaque tells of John de Narde, French prisoner from the Napoleonic War, who escaped from the tower but was later shot and buried in the churchyard.

Near the church is an ancient building, Bishop Bonner's cottages, now a small museum. The thatched building is particularly interesting because of the intricate vine frieze painted around the top of its walls.

(63) EAST DEREHAM

BAILIFF'S DOWNFALL

Position and access: Town sign, centre of East Dereham

OS map reference: TF 989130

This is another Harry Carter sign (see (50) Anmer: Boy Scout and Roman Soldier), and he really excelled himself this time. The carved wooden banner stretches across the street on the southern approach to the town centre, and depicts a legend of St Withburga (see (62) East Dereham: St Withburga's Well).

The story begins when workers building a church required food and drink, but only had a few dry crusts of bread. Withburga prayed to the Virgin Mary, who appeared in a vision and told her to go to the other bank of a nearby stream. Withburga obeyed and found a herd of does that she milked to provide nourishment for the builders. The Town Bailiff, the bad guy of the tale, heard about the miracle and fancied a bit of venison, but when he set off to hunt the deer, his horse fell at a fence and broke its neck. This final dramatic scene is depicted on the two-sided town sign.

Like many old myths, this is probably based on a true event, but the line between fact and fiction has become blurred with time.

Dereham Rotary Club commissioned and paid for the sign in 1954.

(64) SWAFFHAM
GIANT WIND TURBINE

Position and access:	EcoTech Discovery Centre, north Swaffham, near the junction of the A1065 with the A47.
OS map reference:	TF 817098

This is the UK's largest wind turbine, and the only one with a viewing gallery. Sixty-seven metres high, it stands taller than the Statue of Liberty. Anyone climbing the three hundred steps to the gallery is rewarded with a fantastic panorama of East Anglia. The turbine can generate up to 1,500,000 Watts of power, quietly and cleanly, and supplies Swaffham with about a third of its electricity.

EcoTech opened in 1998 as an environmental exhibition centre, and the turbine began generating electricity on Monday 16th August 1999. Interactive displays show the history of the world, how mankind affects the environment and what we can do to help preserve it. The award winning EcoTech building was designed to save energy, with rainwater recycling and computerised temperature control. There is an organic garden in the grounds, tended by local volunteers.

(65) EAST LEXHAM
OLDEST SAXON ROUND TOWER

Position and access:	From Swaffham, take the A1065 north for about 5 miles, then turn right to East Lexham. In the village, turn left, then right towards Lexham. St Andrew's church is on the right.
OS map:	Landranger 132; grid ref. TF 860172

Churches with round towers are exclusive to Norfolk and Suffolk, at least in Britain, and there are nearly two hundred of them. The oldest ones date from Saxon times, although some of the later ones are Norman. There is even a Round Tower Churches Society, made up of people who are interested in this aspect of church history. (See also (55) Little Snoring: Detached Church Tower.)

St Andrew's church, just north of East Lexham village, has one of the oldest round towers, and some historians believe it is the very oldest, the forerunner of the rest.

The tower's position is as intriguing as its age. St Andrew's is part of a little group of four Anglo-Saxon churches; the others are those at Newton-by-Castle Acre, West Lexham and Great Dunham (although West Lexham church was in ruins by 1891, according to a picture inside the church, and later was reconstructed). These four churches were untouched by the widespread Norman re-building of churches that affected most of Norfolk, possibly because of the protection of nearby Castle Acre monastery, which is now itself in ruins.

East Lexham is set in the picturesque Nar Valley and is near the Norfolk Wildlife Trust's Litcham Common Nature Reserve.

(66) BITTERING
WOODLAND SHRINE

Position and access:	From East Dereham, take the B1110 northwards. Fork left on the B1146 through Beetley, then turn left to Bittering. In the village turn right, left and left again. The shrine is in Spread Oak Wood on your left, and is accessed by turning left into the gravel works and backtracking along the trail to your right, along the wood's edge. The shrine is just inside the wood.
OS map reference:	TF 934173

This little chapel, dedicated to the Virgin Mary, was built by Paul Hodac, a Czechoslovakian soldier who fought in World War 2. Mr Hodac's military career began in March 1938 when the young forestry worker enlisted to defend his homeland from the Nazis. When Hitler's troops invaded Czechoslovakia, Mr Hodac took a great risk and escaped to Poland, having first prayed to the Virgin Mary for safety in the crossing. As the invading army moved across Europe, he fought on the front line and ended up in England when France fell to the Germans.

After the war, he never forgot his escape from the Nazis and decided to build a shrine as a gesture of thanks to the Virgin Mary, where people could come and pray. He bought Spread Oak Wood, an isolated and peaceful site, for this purpose. Mr Hodac then taught himself joinery and bricklaying, and took seven years to build the chapel, mainly at weekends and holidays from work. His only help was in laying the roof beams. As his work became known, people donated items for the chapel. These included the wrought iron gates at the entrance to the shrine grounds, the medieval wooden door, and the internal furniture and religious adornments. The stone arch around the door came from Kempstone church, near Litcham. A cross-stitch picture of roses in an urn was made by soldiers waiting in the trenches during the first world war.

The shrine opened in 1983 and mass is held there annually. People from all denomination are welcome. For the rest of the year, the chapel stands alone in its quiet woodland surroundings, a fitting memorial to the Czech airmen based at Wretham Airfield during the war.

PAIR OF SUNDIALS

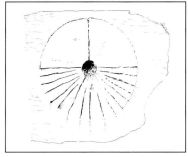
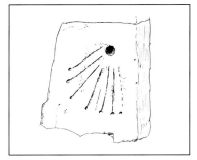

Position and access:	Either side of the porch, St Madeline's Church, Old Beetley. From East Dereham, go north along the B1110, then fork left towards Beetley. Go through the village, then turn right at the crossroads to Old Beetley; the church is to the left on the far side of the road.
OS map reference:	TF 974186

Easily overlooked unless you know they are there, these two small sundials are scratched into the stone, one each side of the porch door. Presumably when they were made, their south-facing position was more open, but now they are shaded by trees for much of the time, except around midday in summer. Even when the sun manages to shine on them, the sundials are no use now, because their gnomons are missing; there are only holes where they used to be.

It is strange that the sun dials were sited on the porch, and not on the tower or some other high spot. They almost look like doodlings or graffiti, but it is not known who put them there, or why.

This small church is Saxon, with a parapet added to the tower in 1911 and paid for by selling oak trees in the churchyard. The village name Beetley comes from Bietel-lea; bietels were wooden mallets used to drive in stakes for stockades or church supports.

(68) NORTH ELMHAM

SAXON CATHEDRAL

Position and access:	From East Dereham, take the B1110 north to North Elmham. The ruined cathedral is through a gateway near the church; it is sign-posted.
OS map reference:	TF 988217

North Elmham was once the centre of Christianity in East Anglia centre, and St Edmund may have been crowned king at the cathedral that once stood here. Although laid waste by the Danes in 866, the bishopric was re-established in 955 until it was moved to Thetford in 1071, and later to Norwich.

Now managed by North Elmham Parish Council in co-operation with English Heritage, the site has been excavated to reveal extensive ruins of various ages. Information boards have been erected telling of its history.

The original timber church was pulled down in 1100 when the nearby parish church was built. A private stone chapel was then built for Bishop Herbert de Losinga of Norwich (see also (2) Norwich: Bishop's Throne). In the late fourteenth century this was converted into a mansion for the then Bishop of Norwich Henry le Despencer, and it remained in use until the 16th century, when it was abandoned and fell into disrepair. The building was obviously well fortified and surrounded by a moat.

(69) SHIPDHAM

ORNATE CUPOLA

Position and access: All Saints' Church in the centre of
Shipdham. From East Dereham, take the
A1075 south-west to Shipdham.

OS map reference: TF 958074

This oak cupola, covered with lead, was added to the church tower
in the early sixteenth century. It is very ornate, with pinnacles and
flying buttresses. In the top dome there is a small medieval bell which
strikes every hour, operated by the large, blue-faced eighteenth century
clock.

The fancy cupola and clock look out of place on this plain
thirteenth century tower. The flint battlements and the west door were
probably added two hundred years later.

All Saints' church was built in the thirteenth century on the site
of an earlier and smaller Norman church.

(70) CARBROOKE
MILLENNIUM GREEN

Position and access:	From Watton, take the minor road heading north-east to Carbrooke. The Millennium Green is on the left of the main village road, opposite the church; the entrance is at the side of a garage.

OS map reference:	TF 947023

Planning for Carbrooke Village Millennium Green began in 1977 and, with help from Millennium Commission funding, a ten acre field was purchased in March 1998 and work began to convert it into an attractive area for people and wildlife. The project was officially opened in September 2000. It is one of 250 millennium greens in England, and the first to be completed.

The green includes over three thousand native trees and shrubs, wildflower areas, a wildlife pond, a Norfolk heritage orchard, a grass amphitheatre, a dogwood and willow maze, and play areas. On entering the site, the most noticeable features are the sculptures: flint toadstools and oak animals.

Wildlife soon moved in. The pond is now home for toads, frogs and newts. Many varieties of dragonflies and butterflies, some rare, have been recorded, as well as green woodpeckers, swallows and kingfishers.

The green is owned by the village and maintained by a charitable trust.

(71) WATTON
FIRE ALARM CLOCK TOWER

Position and access: Tourist Information Office, High Street, Watton, next to town sign.

OS map reference: TF 914008

This narrow building looks out of place between the more modern shop fronts of Watton High Street. It was built by Christopher Hey in 1679, to house a fire alarm bell after a great town fire in the 1670s.

The original clock was probably set in the square recess above the doors, but was replaced in 1827 with a more modern one, donated to the town by Watton citizen Edward Stevens. This has a large mechanism housed in the upper storey. Two large weights take a week to fall from the eaves to just below the lower floor level, driving the timing and striking mechanisms respectively.

This replacement clock face, which was painted with gold numbers and hands, was itself replaced with the present one in 1935 to mark George V's silver jubilee.

The bell, which is struck on the whole hour, hangs outside in the cupola on top of the building. It was cast in 1835 and is about 45 cm in diameter. It was commissioned to commemorate Edwards Stevens' serving thirty-nine years as churchwarden.

The brick building was rendered with cement when the first clock was replaced in 1827.

The hare and barrel motif on the tower and weather vane was once part of Watton's insignia, depicted on the original market cross in the market square before Victorian times.

Over the years, the clock tower has had several uses, including cells for lawbreakers, and a rubbish store. In the 1980s, the Town Council had the clock face and mechanism cleaned and overhauled. The inside of the ground floor was refurbished in 1990 to house the Tourist Information Office. In the street in front of the tower, replacing the old town pump, is the town sign depicting the babes in the wood (see (72) Wayland Wood: Remnant of the Wildwood).

(72) WAYLAND WOOD

REMNANT OF THE WILDWOOD

Position and access: From Watton go south on the A1075 towards Thetford. Wayland Wood, a Norfolk Wildlife Trust nature reserve, is on the left after about a mile. Dogs are not allowed in the nature reserve, which is open at all times.

OS map reference: TL 925997

From the road Wayland Wood looks like any other tangled copse. This wood, however, is extremely important, for part of it is a rare surviving remnant of the prehistoric wildwood that colonised the land after the last Ice Age 10 000 years ago.

The name 'Wayland' is derived from the Viking 'Wandund', meaning sacred grove, suggesting that the site may have been used for worship in the ninth century. Two hundred years later Wayland

Wood was recorded in the Domesday Book. Ridges and ditches, remnants of medieval boundaries, still survive. Fourteenth century records show that the wood was then owned by the de Grey family and was an important local source of timber. From medieval times the wood was managed commercially as a coppice, with standard oaks and ashes.

It was during the de Grey's ownership that Wayland Wood's most infamous claim to fame originated: the 'babes-in-the-woods' affair. According to this folk tale, two orphaned children were taken into the wood to be murdered by order of their wicked uncle, who probably stood to gain their inheritance. One of the hired killers, however, took pity on the children, killed his partner and let the children go. Unlike the pantomime, the legend ends tragically with the children lying down to sleep under an oak, where they died of cold.

It is likely that this story was inspired by real events, and it is commemorated in a carved wooden fireplace in nearby Griston Hall, and on Griston village sign (see (73) Griston: Babes-in-the-Woods Sign). Locals say that ghostly cries may be heard at night, giving the wood its alternative local name of Wailing Wood.

Having survived so long, Wayland Wood was almost lost in the 1940s. During the war the wood was due to be cleared to make way for an aerodrome but, fortunately, this never happened. The wood was badly damaged immediately after the war when bulldozers arrived to take out the standard oaks, crushing much of the understorey in the process. Since then the wood was largely neglected until it was purchased by the Norfolk Naturalists Trust (now the Norfolk Wildlife Trust) for a nature reserve. The NWT has restored the wood to its traditional coppice with standards, which allows a rich variety of spring wildflowers to grow and encourage butterflies and birds. It is the only site in Norfolk where the yellow star of Bethlehem, which flowers in March, can be found.

(73) GRISTON

BABES-IN-THE-WOODS SIGN

Position and access: From Watton, take the A1075 south-east
and turn left to Griston. The sign is in the
village centre near the church and pub.

OS map reference: TL 943994

    This colourful and dramatic scene depicts the tale of the babes-
in-the-woods, believed to have taken place for real in nearby Wayland
Wood (see (72) Wayland Wood: Remnant of the Wildwood for the
full story). It was carved by prolific sign-maker Harry Carter (see also
(50) Anmer: Boy Scout and Roman Soldier).

(74) THOMPSON COMMON

PINGOS

Position and access: From Watton take the A1075 south towards
Thetford. About 3 miles on, just past the
second turn-off to Thompson on the right,
is Thompson Common car park.

OS map reference: TL 940967

A notice board in the car park informs visitors that they are about
to enter "The Great Eastern Pingo Trail". This display contains
information on the history of the area and its wildlife.

Pingos are shallow circular pools formed during the retreat of the
last Ice Age around 10 000 years ago. They developed from small
hillocks formed when underground water froze and pushed the soil
upwards. In the short summers the ice partly thawed and water ran
off the slopes. When the ice finally melted, the mounds collapsed to
form water-filled craters.

There used to be a belt of pingos where the ice sheet ended but, apart from a few isolated examples, the Pingo Trail pools are the only ones left. These rare ponds are important conservation features, home to aquatic plants such as bog-bean, water violet and water bistort. Many dragonfly species breed in them, including the emerald damselfly which was thought to be extinct until rediscovered here. Frogs, newts and water beetles also inhabit the pingos, and the larger pools are visited by wintering wildfowl.

Thompson Common, owned and managed by Norfolk Wildlife Trust (NWT), contains a mixture of habitats as well as the pingos. Much of it is woodland, with scrub and meadow areas. Like most nature reserves, Thompson Common is unstable, needing constant attention to prevent its reversion to dense woodland. Since common grazing ceased in the middle of the twentieth century, scrub and trees have multiplied, endangering the grassland and pingos with their precious wildlife. NWT staff and volunteers are constantly working to preserve this important site.

The "Pingo Trail" is an eight mile walk through Thompson Common and neighbouring areas. It was set up by Norfolk County Council with help from the Countryside Commission and the Manpower Services Commission.

(75) WYMONDHAM

ABBEY WITH TWO TOWERS

Access: From Wymondham town centre, go down
                                 Market Street, turn left at the library, then
                                 left at the aptly named Vicar Street.

OS map reference: TG 106015

   This partly ruined abbey has a history of decidedly un-Christian
disagreements between monks and laity. Founded in 1107 by William
d'Albini, Henry I's chief butler, Wymondham Abbey was dedicated
to the Virgin Mary and St Alban. Later this was changed to St Mary
and St Thomas of Canterbury.

   The two huge towers resulted from a falling out between town
and tonsure, which lasted for centuries and at times became violent.
In 1249 the Pope intervened in an unsuccessful attempt to bring peace,
and 200 years later the Archbishop of Canterbury tried likewise. The
Benedictine monks built the octagonal tower and put up a wall to
prevent the townsfolk from seeing the high altar. The townspeople
retaliated by building for themselves the larger square tower. Even
then the arguments continued, this time over whose bells should go
in which tower.

   The monks' end has mostly disappeared and their tower is a ruin,
courtesy of Henry VIII's Reformation.

   Wymondham Abbey is still in use as the parish church and concert
venue. It overlooks the Tiffey Valley river walk and conservation area.

(76) WYMONDHAM

MARKET CROSS

Position and access: Wymondham town centre.

OS map reference: TG 102015

This stilted octagonal building stands at the very centre of Wymondham. The site originally held a simple cross on a stepped base. Thomas Walsingham, Prior of Wymondham from 1394 to 1400, recorded that miracles happened by Wymondham Cross in 1389, but did not specify what they were. At some time a building replaced the cross, but this and many other buildings burnt down in 1615.

The present building was built in 1916 at a cost of £25.7s, and renovated in 1989 for almost £95,000. Accessed by an external wooden staircase, it now houses Wymondham Tourist Information Centre.

(77) WYMONDHAM

MOOT HILL

Position and access:	This is easy to see but difficult to get to. It lies alongside the A11 dual carriageway but there is nowhere to stop. If you park at Kett's Park Recreation Centre, London Road (near Norfolk Constabulary HQ), Wymondham, you can walk across the field to the small fenced wood to the south.
OS map reference:	TG 125018

This is not a hill by any stretch of the imagination, and it looks like just another small copse surrounded by fields, but its dense trees hide an enigma. Inside the wood is an oval earthwork, consisting of a ditch and low rampart surrounding a relatively open space.

No-one knows for sure what used to occupy the site. Theories include a Norman fortress, a meeting place or "moot", a theatre for medieval mystery plays, or a medieval manor house.

KETT'S OAK

Position and access:	On the old Norwich Road, half way between Wymondham and Hethersett. From Wymondham, the tree is by a lay-by on the left, opposite a mile stone on the right of the road.
OS map reference:	TG 138036

This ancient oak would have toppled over long ago if it had not been bound with iron bands and held up by wooden props. Its massive trunk is split vertically, and the crack has been filled with concrete, presumably to slow the decay of the wood. Unlike most ancient oaks, it supports very little ivy, but that is probably because the climber is pulled off when it gets too rampant. The tree is surrounded by a metal fence with the sign: "Kett's Oak, 1549".

This oak is said to mark the spot where rebel leader Robert Kett of Wymondham made a speech to his followers before they marched on Norwich. It is not known whether the oak was planted in memory of Kett, or was already there when he orated to the rebels, in which case it could be even older than four and a half centuries.

The 1549 Ketts' Rebellion, headed by Robert and his brother William, was part of a nation-wide revolution against enclosure of common land by landowners. This was no mere protest march; it was more like a civil war. The Ketts and a large band of rebels - about twenty thousand men and women - camped on Mousehold Heath outside Norwich, then stormed and captured the walled city with much loss of life. They imprisoned the mayor, Thomas Cod, and replaced him with Austin Steward who was sympathetic to the cause. The rebels fought off the Marquis of Northampton's army of 1500 men.

It eventually took12 000 soldiers, led by the Earl of Warwick, to retake Norwich. The Ketts fled but were captured, and were hanged on the 7th of December 1549. Robert Kett was hanged from the walls of Norwich Castle, and his brother from Wymondham Abbey tower.

The Ketts and their followers are now honoured as heroes. Four centuries after the rebellion, a memorial plaque was placed at Robert Kett's execution site. It reads: "In 1549 AD Robert Kett, Yeoman of Wymondham, was executed by hanging in this castle after the defeat of the Norfolk Rebellion of which he was the leader. In 1949 AD, four hundred years later, this memorial was placed here by the citizens of Norwich in reparation and honour to a notable and courageous leader in the long struggle of the common people of England to escape from a servile life into the freedom of just condition".

(79) ATTLEBOROUGH
PYRAMID

Position and access:	In Attleborough Cemetery, accessed from the back of the main town car park. The pyramid is near the chapel.
OS map reference:	TM 047958

Incongruous among the tombstones, this 1.8 metre high limestone structure marks the final resting place of Melancthon William Henry 'Lawyer' Brook, buried in 1929. Although not as large and grand as the Blickling pyramid (see (34) Blickling: Pyramid), it is still impressive amongst the more conventional tombstones. The Norfolk solicitor left detailed instructions in his will for his memorial, including its exact measurements and material. Perhaps suspecting that his wishes would not be taken seriously, he endowed a library to the town, but only if his pyramid was built and looked after.

Brook's will also reveals a domestic dispute between master and servant. He left £20 to his housekeeper, Florence Curtis, although the lady would have received £100 "if she had complied with my wishes and continued to wear for service the white cap and apron which became her so well". The lawyer relented, however, and added a codicil raising the bequest to £50.

116

(80) LITTLE ELLINGHAM
CLOCK TOWER COTTAGES

Position and access: From Attleborough, take the B1077 to
Great Ellingham. In the village, turn left at
the second crossroads, then second left to
Little Ellingham. Follow the road through
the village. The clock tower is on the right
of the drive to Little Ellingham Hall.

OS map reference: TM 003994

This is an unexpected curiosity in a small rural village: a tall, square clock tower surrounded by four cottages with massive chimneys. It was built around 1855, the same time as the hall in whose grounds it stands, but I cannot find the name of the innovative designer.

One side of the tower holds a large clock face, but there are only blank, bricked-in circles on the other three facets. Whether there used to be clocks on all four sides, or whether the intention was to have four clocks but funding ran out, is anyone's guess. The remaining clock is now in poor condition, and looks like it stopped working long ago.

A small top storey above the clock has louvered doors, and above that is a domed roof.

The cottages, one each side around the tower's base and joined to form a cross shape, were built for the estate's gardeners. Now one of them is a private residence, with a well tended garden. The rest appear to be used for storage.

(81) ROCKLAND

ST ANDREW'S RUIN

Position and access: From Attleborough, take the B1077
through Great Ellingham. At Rockland
crossroad turn left, fork right then left,
then turn left towards the square-towered
church of All Saints'. St Andrew's ruined
tower is a little further on, by the right
side of the road.

OS map reference: TL 996959

Rockland has three churches, but unlike those at Reepham (see
(57) Reepham: Three Churches in One Churchyard), these are
scattered. The village is split into two parishes: Rockland St Peter with
a round-towered church, and Rockland All Saints with a square-
towered church, both still in use. There used to be a third, Rockland
St Andrew, but all that remains of their church is part of the old tower.
The ruin is near All Saints' Church, so presumably the local population
found they did not need two churches and the parishes merged.

St Andrew's tower is imposing when you first come across it. It
is cracked and fissured, and overgrown with creepers which look like
they are holding it together.

St Andrew's ruin and All Saints church, together with a small brick
building that was erected in 1845 as a schoolhouse, are set apart from
the main part of Rockland All Saints village. Churches in the middle
of the countryside, well away from habitations, are a common sight
in Norfolk.

(82) THETFORD

CASTLE MOUND

Position and access: Castle Street, south-east of Thetford town centre.

OS map reference: TL 874828

This incredibly steep mound, which children - and some adults - love to climb, is the tallest earthwork in Britain. An information board near the mound describes the site's history.

There are remains of two ruined structures here: an Iron Age fort and a Norman castle. Iceni Queen Boadicea's (also called Boudica) ancestors built the first fortification around 500 BC, and two great banks and ditches remain. Thetford was then a tribal centre of the Iceni. They sited their fort strategically, overlooking the Icknield Way and two fords over the Rivers Thet and Little Ouse. The Iceni therefore controlled the major land and river routes.

The twenty-four metre high mound later had a wooden Norman castle on top, built inside the Iron Age fort remains. In the 1070s Thetford was the sixth largest town in England, and Ralph Guader was Earl of East Anglia. The earl led a revolt in 1075 against William the Conqueror, however, and was replaced by Roger Bigod who also founded the Priory of St Mary (see (83) Thetford: Ruined Priory). It is not known which of these two earls built the castle.

The fortress was a motte and bailey type (that is, a mound surrounded by banks and ditches). It would have included store houses, workshops, barracks and animal sheds.

The castle mound is made from the chalk sub-soil excavated from the ditches, and there are white streaks where chalk is exposed. The site is freely accessible, and is used as a leisure and play area. Part of the field is managed as a meadow, where a rich variety of chalk grassland wildflowers grow.

(83) THETFORD
RUINED PRIORY

Position and access:	Near London Road, west of Thetford town centre. It is well signposted and there is a car park.
OS map reference:	TL 865834

These extensive ruins were once an important Cluniac Priory, built in 1107 by Roger Bigod, Earl of Norfolk. Henry I laid the foundation stone with great ceremony. The buildings were extended and added to over the centuries. Visitors can wander freely amongst the ruins, and there are several information boards and signs scattered about this English Heritage site.

The priory church was half as big as Norwich Cathedral, and was surrounded by cloisters, Prior's lodgings, a Lady Chapel and the gatehouse.

Priories were built as off-shoots of Abbeys. The first monks to settle at Thetford came from Lewes Priory, Sussex, itself an off-shoot of the great Cluny Abbey in France. Occasionally the prior was summoned to attend a meeting at Cluny, a long and arduous journey.

In medieval times the monastery was entered via the splendid fourteenth century gatehouse, at the opposite end of the site to the present entrance. The gatehouse is set apart from the rest of the priory, on private ground, but can be visited during opening hours. This square building is now full of pigeons roosting on its high ledges. There is a round tower in one corner, containing the remains of a spiral staircase.

The priory's end came with Henry VIII's dissolution of the monasteries. He sold the buildings to the Duke of Norfolk, who pulled down some of them and sold the stones. Over the following years the rest of the priory fell into ruins and its stones ended up in many buildings in and around Thetford, including the Warren Lodge (see (84) Thetford: Warren Lodge).

(84) THETFORD

WARREN LODGE

Position and access:	From Thetford, take the B1107 towards Brandon. The Lodge is well signed, on the left about two miles from Thetford. There is a car park.
OS map reference:	TL 839841

The walk from the car park to the Lodge feels more like trekking through dunes than forest. The earth is pure sand, and it is hard going.

The Warren Lodge stands a short way into mixed woodland. It is a cubic, flint building that has been there since the fifteenth century. The walls are crumbling and the lodge is now fenced off, preventing visitors from getting too close.

It was built as a house and headquarters for the gamekeeper of the Prior of Thetford, who had hunting rights in this part of the forest. He would catch rabbits by netting, and also used ferrets and lurcher dogs. Another way was to dig eight feet deep "pitfall" traps; over each trap was a swivel door baited with hay. The hunting was sustainable, with the gamekeeper allowed to catch ten rabbits per acre per year.

Rabbits were introduced to Breckland by the Normans, who kept them in warrens and farmed them for meat and fur. Rabbit farming was a local occupation up to World War 2.

An information panel by the Lodge states that it is an English Heritage site. Norfolk Heritage, a voluntary organisation, helps with the upkeep, choosing the Lodge as one of a series of sites to illustrate the theme "Food from the Land".

(85) EAST WRETHAM HEATH
DISAPPEARING MERES

Position and access: East Wretham Heath Nature Reserve, west side of the A1075, five miles north-east of Thetford.

OS map reference: TL 906885 and 909879

Whether you see the two small lakes of Langmere and Ringmere depends on when you visit. Their levels have always fluctuated, normally being higher in summer after the winter rains, and low or even dried up in winter after the summer drought. These fluctuations are by no means regular, and during prolonged dry spells, the water may disappear for several years running. This last happened around 1995 to 1998. With increased extraction of Breckland's ground water it was feared that the meres had gone for good, and dense vegetation colonised their beds. The following winter was back to normal, however, and the meres soon filled up again, to the delight of local birds - and bird watchers who use the hide overlooking Langmere.

The meres have no obvious inlets or outlets, and probably originated from small, water-filled hollows in the chalk bedrock which gradually dissolved away.

These lakes are part of Norfolk Wildlife Trust's (NWT) East Wretham Heath Nature Reserve, which contains a number of other interesting features and habitats. Part of the reserve was a World War 2 airfield, and remains of the runways and buildings support colonies of mosses, lichens and wildflowers of dry places. A considerably older habitat is a pine plantation dating from the time of the Napoleonic Wars. Deciduous woodland and heathland support many plants and animals.

Alongside the track leading between the two meres, there is a memorial stone to Dr Sydney Long, 1870-1939, the founder of the NWT (then called the Norfolk Naturalists Trust) in 1926.

East Wretham Heath is open daily, with free admittance. There are nature trails, including one for visually handicapped people.

(86) QUIDENHAM
VIKING'S MOUND

Position and access:	From Thetford, take the A11 north-east towards Attleborough. Turn right at the staggered crossroad signed to East Harling, then left to Quidenham. Turn left at the junction. Viking's Mound is on the left, just past the church; it is reached by walking a short way up a track, then climbing up on to the mound.
OS map reference:	TM 026878

Legend has it that Queen Boadicea is buried here - but three other places in Norfolk make the same claim! The myth probably originated from one of her battles in the region. A large number of bones have been found in the churchyard, jumbled up as though fallen in battle.

In reality, Viking's Mound had nothing to do with the Vikings or Boadicea, but was almost certainly the site of a Norman fortification.

From the road the Mound looks like a small wood on a low hill, backed by a fir plantation. You need to climb up to the circle of oaks on top to appreciate this ancient site, surrounded by a circular ditch.

The village hall has a heritage map on its outside wall, with lots of information about Quidenham and the surrounding area. Continuing the Boadicea theme, the village sign shows the queen in her chariot, pulled by two fine horses. This sign was designed by a villager, Mrs P MacNamara, and presented by the ladies of the Boadicea Club, with contributions from Quidenham Parish Council and the village.

(87) QUIDENHAM
HYBRID CHURCH TOWER

Position and access: For directions to Quidenham, see (85) Quidenham: Viking's Mound. St Andrew's Church is at the south end of the village.

OS map reference: TM 028877

St Andrew's Church, Quidenham, is an attractive flint church with a curious tower that has obviously been added to more than once. Although many churches have been modified and added to over the years, the three main sections of this tower have obviously distinct styles.

The lower round tower, like many similar ones in Norfolk, is Saxon, dating from around 950-1050 (see also (65) East Lexham: Oldest Saxon Round Tower). Four centuries later, the octagonal bell tower was built on top, with battlements and belfry windows. The builders of that time included a flint spire, but this was replaced with the present spire in 1857. The top of the spire was replaced in 1930, costing £180 which was raised by an appeal. Later restoration was carried out in 1989 by local craftsman George Padgett, for £45 000.

The lower walls of the tower are over a metre thick, and the whole tower is twenty-four metres high. The clock was made in 1861 by Tucker of London, and chimes were added in 1902. The chimes do not work now, but the parishioners are raising funds for repairs to the clock and tower.

The inside of the church is as interesting as the outside, with some beautiful stained glass windows. You can look up inside the hollow Saxon tower, with its dangling bell ropes. A small chapel on the right of the church is dedicated to the 96th Bomber Group, who were stationed at nearby Snetterton Airfield. Servicemen of the 96th donated the £600 cost of the chapel in memory of their colleagues who were killed in action. This was the first WW2 memorial chapel in England.

(88) GARBOLDISHAM
PLEACHED TREES

Position and access:	From Diss take the A1066 westwards towards Thetford. On reaching Garboldisham, turn right on to the B1114 towards Attleborough. The memorial and pleached trees are ahead on the left.
OS map reference:	TM 006007

Most villages have a war memorial, but this one is unusual in being surrounded by a "hedge on stilts", a beautifully tended row of pleached trees.

Pleaching is a way of pruning trees to form an aerial hedgerow supported by bare trunks, and can be seen in certain large formal gardens such as the National Trust's Hidcote Manor Garden in Gloucestershire. It is very rare to find pleached trees outside of gardens.

Garboldisham is a large village with an attractive church and other buildings. A couple of miles to the west, the Anglo-Saxon Devil's Ditch crosses the main road, although it is not easy to see at this point.

(89) THE TIVETSHALLS
METAL VILLAGE SIGN

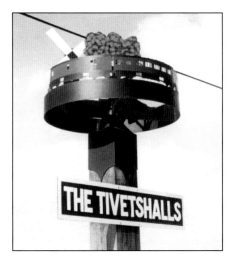

Position and access: From Diss, take the A140 north towards Norwich. At the B1134 crossroad turn left, take the next left on to Star Street and follow the road round a few bends until you reach a T-junction. Turn right, and the village hall and sign are about 100 metres on your left.

OS map reference: TM   168867

Several villages commissioned new village signs to commemorate the millennium, and that of the Tivetshalls (Tivetshall St Margaret and Tivetshall St Mary) is one of the most unusual. This metal sign, featuring a steam train on a circular track surrounding a windmill, was designed by Steve Eggleton from Banham and made by blacksmith David Butler, resident of Tivetshall St Mary.

The sign was unveiled by two residents in July 2000, as part of a weekend of festivities organised by Tivetshall Parish Council. Proceeds were donated to local good causes, including the Eastern Daily Press's 'We Care 2000' appeal, set up to help people caring for ill and disabled relatives.

(90) PULHAM ST MARY
AIRSHIP SIGN

Position and access:	From Diss, take the A143 east, then turn left on to the A140 towards Norwich. Go right at the crossroad with the B1134 to Pulham St Mary. The sign is in the centre of the village, at a road junction near the pub.
OS map reference:	TM 210853

This splendid village sign depicts an airship, the R-33 at its mooring mast. Pulham's association with airships began during World War 1, when 'blimps' of the Royal Navy Air Service arrived at a nearby air base. The locals called the airships 'Pulham pigs' because of their shape. During and after the war, airships of a variety of sizes and shapes were based at Pulham. They were used mainly to patrol the coast and as escorts. Airships flew from Pulham throughout the 1920s, but after the R-101 disaster in 1930, Britain's airship programme was abandoned and Pulham Air Base fell into disuse until World War 2.

The R-33 airship first flew in March 1919, and took part in the victory celebrations over London in June of that year. Over the next eight years it took part in several historic flights, including a round trip of nine hundred miles to Dublin and the Isle of Man in July 1919, but was scrapped in 1928. The forward section of its control car is on display at the RAF Museum, Hendon.

BIBLIOGRAPHY

Ivan Bunn and M Burgess, *Local Curiosities*, 1976

T K Cromwell, *Excursions in the County of Norfolk*, Longham 1818

Gwyn Headley and Wim Meulenkamp, *Follies: a National Trust guide*, Cape 1986

Gwyn Headley, *Follies, grottoes and garden buildings*, Aurum 1999

Rick O'Brien, *East Anglian Curiosities: a guide to follies and strange buildings, curious tales and unusual people*, Dovecote Press 1992

Keith Skipper, *Hidden Norfolk*, Countryside Books 1998

John Timpson, *Timpson's England: a look beyond the obvious at the unusual, the eccentric and the definitely odd*, Jarrold 1987

John Timpson, *Timpson's Towns of England and Wales: oddities and curiosities*, Jarrold 1989

John Timpson, *Timpson's Country Churches*, Weidenfield 1998

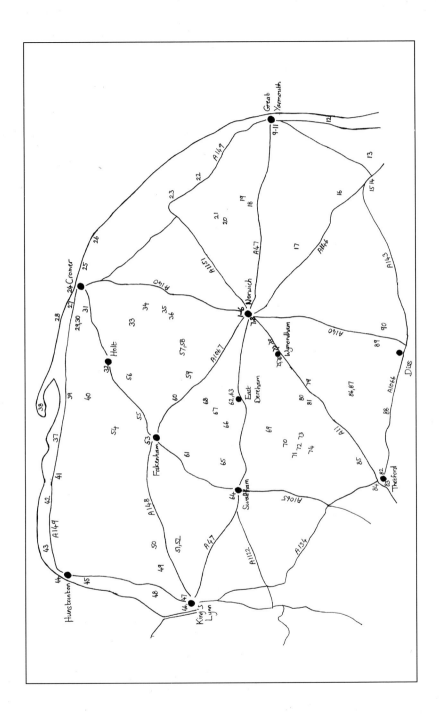